Your Powerful

*To The*

Boo

# NABSE & ME
# The National Alliance of Black
# School Educators

*A Leader's Quest to Save Every*
*Child But Loses His Own Son*

Bernard Hamilton, Jr.

Published by **To The Point**
Next Stage Communications
A Subsidiary of Next Stage Speaking

Next Stage Communications
3638 Tioga Way
Las Vegas, NV 89169
(702) 682-8431

ISBN: 978-1-7338602-8-4

Bernard Hamilton Jr.

## Contents

NABSE And Me

# Prologue

Self-esteem and positive role models are critical for a young boy. I know, because I did not have either as a youngster. I didn't believe in myself. I had low self-esteem. I know what that feels like, and I know how debilitating that can be. Still, I managed to find my way, and I'm thankful for that.

My upbringing in the South brought episodes that have stayed with me for the length of my life. The world was different back then. Everything moved a little slower, and progress in the way of civil rights had not been made. Yet most of my problems as a child stemmed from an abusive stepfather, who had alcohol issues and wasn't equipped to extend to me a much-desired helping hand. What I would have done for just one word of encouragement, or even an acknowledgement of my existence. Those words or gestures never came.

While I look back at my childhood with sadness, what I endured opened my eyes to how not to raise a child, and what a child needed. That base of knowledge served as a bridge to my life's work, which has been to implement the goals of the National Alliance of Black School Educators (NABSE) and its mission to save the children of African descent.

NABSE became a route for me to explore my journey, opening my eyes to the fact I wasn't by myself on this mission. I felt strongly about this mission even as a youngster. I realized that my upbringing and what I endured as a youngster fuel the message in which I believed.

Everything clicked the first time I got introduced to NABSE. I said, "Oh my goodness, we've got people across the country educating families and kids, with the idea that everybody can learn. It's just a matter of will."

My introduction to NABSE came while I was serving in many organizations. The fact that NABSE had affiliates across the country meant a lot to me. I began to meet NABSE chapter presidents nationwide who were doing everything necessary to try and make the mission I believed in come to fruition. And I thought how wonderful the possibilities were for doing things across the country. Not just locally.

I worked with NABSE as a member in the 80s, an affiliate president in the three states that my career followed in the 90s, the chair of the National Membership Program, and a founder of new affiliates in the 21st century. I had the pleasure to work with many of NABSE's past presidents and founders. Dr. Charles Moody, long recognized as the original founder of the National Alliance of Black Superintendents, encouraged me to work with Membership. NABSE

President Dr. Charlie Mae Knight asked me to be the chair of Membership. President Dr. Donald Smith came to Las Vegas and encouraged me and others to become more active in NABSE. President Dr. Russell Jackson became not only a mentor but friend and financial advisor. President Dr. Charles Townsel, Dr. Deborah Wolfe, Dr. Patricia Ackerman, Dr. Ted Kimbrough, Dr. Jerome Harris, and Dr. Charles Thomas all encouraged my involvement and were mentors as I worked in NABSE. I was grateful to have served on the NABSE Board with Dr. Knight, Dr. Joseph Drayton, Dr. Lois Harrison Jones, Dr. Andre Hornsby, Dr. Deloris Saunders, Dr. Emma Epps, Dr. Deborah Hunter-Harvill, Dr. Carrol Thomas, Mrs. Marietta English, and the current President Dr. Michael McFarland. As a board member I also served in many capacities, including chair of the Superintendents Commission two terms, Coordinator of Affiliates, and various committee positions.

I have always preached to others the need to go to the national conference in order to energize themselves. Some of the best speakers, and people in general, from around the world attend these conferences. Listening to the message, you get the feeling that things really can change. Some of the speakers and presenters included Professors Linda Darling-Hammond, Asa Hilliard, Cornel West, Robert Peterkin, Charles Ogletree, Charlene Hunter, and Robert Green; Secretaries of Education Arne Duncan, John King, and Rod Paige; authors Michael Eric Dyson, Pedro Noguera, and

Nikki Giovanni; Ambassador Andrew Young; Secretary of Defense Colin Powell; Reverends Jesse Jackson and Al Sharpton; Mayors Cory Booker and Harold Washington; Dr. Ben Carson; and political strategist Donna Brazile.

NABSE was like kindling wood to the fire for me. The organization and what it represented just got me all excited to go out there and make a difference. And I was on a tear for trying to learn more about the strategies that would ensure that every kid could learn and to give them support and a lot of hope.

I was young and just entering the learning curve of trying to educate myself on how to be an administrator. That added excitement to my pursuit. But my hopes weren't just for Black kids. I wanted to save every kid, and still do. A lot of times the solutions aren't complicated. For example, the special education kid. He's sitting in the classroom, obviously he has academic disabilities, maybe even physical disabilities. You don't treat him like everybody else. You try to give him what he needs to make it. If a kid can't read the board, you get the kid glasses. At the same time, you don't ignore the academically talented kid. You give him more advanced material. At my 50th high school reunion, a former classmate and mother of one of my Walter Bracken students told me that I had changed her son's life. I had recognized he was not learning and I provided specialized help for him. She cried and hugged me so tightly. I could feel the gratitude. Her son thanked me and came to the reunion just to show his appreciation. It was another affirmation that we can reach every kid. God gave each of us gifts. And those gifts need to be recognized, and they need to grow. And when they grow, that individual will benefit, as will society. That's NABSE's belief as well as what I preached at Walter Bracken.

NABSE just had so many possibilities that I was sure that this was the organization with which I wanted to be a part and grow. I'd never heard any other organizations say, "We can educate every kid. We know what we need to do, we just need the will."

I've always felt that about most things. If you have the will, you should be able to do it. Will, faith, hope, discipline, that type of thing.

I once gave a boss of mine the book *The Case for Christ*.

I explained to him that I gave him the book not because I questioned his faith, rather because I knew he was helping many kids and put a lot of effort into how much he would try to help. But I told him, "You know what, our goal is not to live to be 110 and say what great things we did while we were here. Our goal is to say, 'You know, I was prepared for eternal life.' That's our goal. So, to that end, we want other folks to enjoy that goal."

NABSE gave me the opportunity to model these Christian values and to discuss "High Achievement for All" not only in my community but in opening up the world starting with all of the USA and eventually being able to discuss both children and adult needs in Nova Scotia, Toronto, Cape Town, Johannesburg, Senegal, Rome, the Bahamas, and Aruba to name a few.

That book has all kinds of evidence and details about how Christ—the son of God—lived, even though they didn't believe in him. But guess what, because they documented that they saw him, they inadvertently proved that the Man lived on earth.

I concluded, "You just don't gloat in your Michael Jordan accomplishments, you provide opportunities for other people."

That's one of my gifts, I guess. I don't disrespect anybody's disability, but I don't over respect anybody's ability. I don't care if you're the president of the United States or the poorest person in the world. We're just going to have a good time talking.

I've always felt like the noblest way to spend one's life is to try and benefit the greater good. I saw that in NABSE. That's why I pursued trying to absorb everything I could that NABSE taught and represented. I was like a sponge. When I came back from NABSE conferences, I would bring back what I'd learned and share it with my staff and colleagues. I would even send it to my boss, the superintendent of schools. My hope was he would share it with other principals. And I did share with a lot of folks.

I believed in NABSE's mission of "Saving the African American Child" as discussed in a 1984 publication by NABSE. I went all out to do that but, I couldn't save my son.

NABSE provided building blocks to me and others regarding child development and needs, but I missed the "Tell Tale" signs of my own child's needs. No matter how professional and educated we are, we are not exempt from tragedy. We can't prevent bad things from knocking at our door.

Though I have enjoyed great professional success in my life—I've overcome a great deal given my background, and NABSE's work has been exemplary—I'm reminded of the book *The Failure of the Black Middle Class*. My rising from poverty to middle class did not help me save my son from having a poor self-concept and following the wrong group of friends. My inability to prevent his nefarious relationship with addictive drug abuse is my biggest regret.

Writing this book has been therapeutic, affording me the opportunity to examine the childhood memories that shaped me. But it has also given me an opportunity to highlight the NABSE's work—unknown by many—along with some of my past successes as an educator.

# CHAPTER ONE

My first memory is Montgomery, Alabama, and the house on Sutter Street where we lived. We had running water, but we didn't have a tub. We bathed out of a white bucket and had to use an outhouse out back, and that was scary because every now and then I'd hear gunshots when I was in the outhouse. From time to time, I had to sleep with my aunt, my mother's only sister, Babette. We never saw Whites in our neighborhood, that was life in the segregated South, but I didn't know anything about the repercussions of segregation at the time. Sitting at the back of the bus and not being able to drink from the "White" water fountain was just a part of life.

Montgomery is the capital of Alabama, and the downtown part of the city is set along the southern bank of the Alabama River. While in Montgomery, I experienced the first miracle in my life at the age of five. That's when I believe God saved me from a fire.

I remember the smoke and the awareness that our one-story house had caught on fire. Like many Southern homes, ours was elevated with a porch. The house had belonged to my grandmother before being passed down to my mother.

With the house engulfed in flames, my first thought was to go outside and yell for help, because I knew it was bad. I could feel the heat. I could see the darkness of the smoke. I couldn't quite get outside. Despite my age—I was just five—I understood the dire circumstances. I might have been anxious, but I don't remember being scared.

Birdie, my younger sister, was inside the house. I knew I had to try and save her. To do so I had to try and wake her up and get her out of the crib.

If I would have been scared, I probably would have been immobilized by the accompanying sense of fear. All I could think about was, "Hey, there's a fire in here, we better get covered up." For whatever reason, I've always thought about what do I do next? That's how I think now, and I think that's how I thought back then. That's the only way I can think of things. It's like a logical thing for me. Later, when I took logic in college, I found the subject so plain and clear to me, like, "That's the way it should be."

Birdie and I were both little. I didn't have the strength to hoist her out of the crib. The situation was more of a "Come on! Come on! We've got to get out of here" type of thing. Then I couldn't go any farther. Maybe it was the coughing. Maybe it was the heat. Who knows. I managed to position Birdie facedown in the crib. When I lay on top of her, I knew the fire controlled our destiny. Simply put: Our fate rested in the hands of God.

I don't know where my mother was when the fire started. Later she said she had gone to the store. She knew she shouldn't have left us alone. By the time she returned from wherever she had been, the house had been swallowed by flames. She was frantic. A small gas heater had malfunctioned to cause the fire. My mother said it was not the first time that house had caught on fire.

We were unconscious when the ambulance arrived. Before we reached St. Jude Hospital, they said we were dead and that it was a waste of time to do anything in the way of heroics. Somehow, they revived us.

The recovery took time. We remained in the hospital for several weeks, mainstays in a large room with rows of beds at a place for Blacks only. That hospital would later serve as a rest stop on Dr. Martin Luther King's historical 54-mile march from Selma to Montgomery in 1965.

Though I had escaped with my life, I had burns all over my head. Those scars would take their toll on my self-esteem for years. And even though I covered Birdie, she had burns on her back. That told me she had probably gotten burned before I reached her.

I've never heard Birdie say much about the fire in later years, though I always teased her about saving her life.

We were damaged by more than a fire at that house on Sutter Street.

After we got out of the hospital, we lived at one of my aunt's houses in Montgomery.

I don't remember my biological father ever living with us. My mother and he got divorced before my first memories.

My real father's name was Bernard. Everybody called him "The Bear" for his booming voice. My mother never talked about him much, but she did tell me they liked to dance, and that he was a good dancer.

By the time I could remember, my real father already lived in Detroit with my stepmother Ernestine, who we called Tina. There, he worked on the assembly line for Buick.

From time to time, my father would come to Alabama, and we would visit with him in Detroit every summer. We never lived with him full-time, though.

I've never figured out how my mother, Eddie Mae, could have been attracted to such an abusive man as my stepfather, Walter O'Neal, who we called "Daddy Walt." My mother has always been pretty. I'm sure that was part of what attracted Daddy Walt to her. They met at a bar. She drank, smoked, and danced back in those days. I think she had led a strict life growing up, so once she got freed, she went a little wild and started partying. My mother and stepfather were married in the house that burned down.

Being a kid when that wedding took place, curiosity drove me to scour the scene afterward like kids do. My scavenger hunt led me to a cup filled with what looked like a half-drunk milkshake. A sweet tooth directed me to dive in, and I did. Only the cup didn't have a milkshake inside, rather mayonnaise. I tried to chug it, and the results weren't pretty. Even though I spit it out, I got sick. I've never been able to stomach mayonnaise since.

Daddy Walt had a slender build and dark skin. But his most distinguishing feature was his voice. He had a booming voice just like my father. I guess my mother had a thing for heavy voices. Seemed like my stepfather was always angry. Angry with us. Angry about his job. Angry about most anything. He wasn't so much anti kids. More like he stayed angry at the world. That sort of thing. I think he grew up without a father and had a strict mother. We would visit his family from time to time in the Montgomery project where they lived. His mother had a heavy voice. Like Big Mama on TV.

Daddy Walt served in the military. He frequently got drunk, mostly after work at the military base. I guess that was military life back then. He never ate with us. I don't know why. In my mind I was just glad that he came home late. I heard he was a good mechanic—he worked on airplanes. I also understood that he never advanced in rank because he went to jail a lot, which was mostly due to the fact he wouldn't take anything from anybody, particularly White folks. We might hear, "He got called a nigger today and he took his knife out at the barber shop, and now he's in jail." Maybe that explained his anger and why he was abusive—verbally and physically. He also had a gambling problem. To his credit, he tried to provide for us and he never drank at home. We never saw alcohol anywhere in the house. That restraint didn't prevent him from being abusive, verbally and physically.

I've had people ask me if I ever asked my real father if we could live with him in Detroit. Interesting enough, we didn't think that way. We might have been influenced by my mother's low opinion of my real father.

You hear stories about Blacks from the South deciding to move to the North seeking to find a better life. That wasn't the case with my father. I think it was more the fact that my stepmother had relatives there.

When we visited Detroit, the city life fascinated us. We never went anywhere except home and school when we were in Montgomery. And there we were in Downtown Detroit, which had so many tall buildings. You didn't see those in Alabama. We found the contrast between Detroit and Montgomery to be striking.

You were surrounded by the city. Big roads and wide streets. Alabama had small roads, or country dirt roads. And Detroit felt huge. The first time we visited, my father and Tina were living in a garage at the back of the house owned by other people, who lived in the house. Some days were scary. We heard a lot of sirens, fire trucks, and police cars all night long. We weren't used to that. Crickets were the only sounds we knew from the night.

They had alleys in the big city, located at the back side of the house. That was scary, too. People were a little more careful about who they talked to in the North. And they made a lot of fun of our Southern accents.

We saw White people in Detroit every now and then. While that was different than Montgomery, it wasn't any big deal to me. I wasn't like, "Oh look, there's White people." I never had that ah-hah moment. Mostly in Detroit we saw Blacks, though. Of course, when my father took me shopping in the Polish neighborhood, it was all White.

Because I grew up poor, people have always asked me if I ever put paper in my shoes to compensate for the holes. I'd say, "Heck yeah, I've had paper in my shoes forever." In Montgomery, I walked barefoot everywhere. All the time. It was no big deal. When I'd go to Detroit, my father would always buy me a pair of shoes at the Polish shoe shop in the Polish neighborhood near Dearborn.

There were different neighborhoods in and around Detroit. If you went to the Polish neighborhood you could get some reasonably priced clothes. I remember getting haircuts with my dad. That was a big outing, and so was the trip to buy shoes. He kept promising to take me to a baseball game, but we never quite made it to see the Detroit Tigers.

My father liked to watch baseball. He watched a lot of baseball games. I'd watch with him and think, "Boy these games are long." And he'd always watch the whole game. He liked sports. He later told me he'd been a golf caddy when he was a young man.

My father and stepmother stayed in that same place in Detroit forever. There really wasn't room for us. But that's all they had. It made me feel lucky we were living a bit better than we thought. Mama said we were lucky to have the benefits of the armed services. Daddy Walt did provide us more than we actually appreciated.

Birdie and I could not stand our stepmother. She wasn't nice to us, though she put up with us. She would get jealous whenever our father gave us anything. Didn't matter what he bought us, she mumbled about it, or made a face. He usually tried to give us things when she wasn't around, and he'd tell us to keep it to ourselves. If he gave us money, he'd tell us to keep it to ourselves. She was bad. She'd send us down the street with a couple of dollars to give to a man, so she could play the numbers. And she was an alcoholic. She drank every night. You never saw her without a drink. Booze always coated her breath.

Unlike living with Daddy Walt and my mother, my real father and my stepmother kept liquor in the house. My father controlled his drinking, reserving it for the weekend, but Tina wasn't wired that way. She was so bad off, she had to have her alcohol, almost like medicine. My father went so far as to keep liquor in the trunk of his car for medicinal purposes. If Tina and he drove anywhere, he'd have to stop from time to time to pour her a little drink.

My real father died at the age of 55 and everybody knew what would happen to Tina after he died, and that came to fruition. She drank every single day. Went right through whatever money my father left her—exactly what he feared. Her liver gave out and she died nine months later.

We had a lot of family in Alabama. And among my family there were a lot of interesting characters, like Anthony Moore, who was an uncle. According to legend, while serving at Alcatraz, he escaped by swimming through those cold and shark-infested San Francisco Bay waters to freedom. He went on to live in Washington state.

We had cousins we were close to and we remained close to them. Dan Harris was my first cousin. We called him Pie. We were like brothers. His father and my father were half brothers. He left Alabama to go to Creighton and he went on to become a Mutual of Omaha lawyer. When he later returned to Alabama, he became a city councilman. A couple of years ago he ran for mayor. My cousin Linda Thompson has become a close friend. Her mother, who we called Aunt Doll, was my favorite relative. She always cooked big meals for Birdie and me when we visited in Montgomery, and later in the city of Detroit when her family moved. Her laugh would make you laugh, and she always talked positive about anything we discussed; she never criticized and her love for us radiated in all she did for us. Her sister lived near her, too, Aunt Sister; we loved her, but we knew she was a little jealous of Aunt Doll.

I had more than one uncle. Harold Hamilton interacted with us a lot. Took us to get ice cream and hamburgers. Occasionally, he'd stuff money in our pockets. He was a wonderful, kind man. Another of my father's brothers, Robert Hamilton, used to shoot rabbits, skin them, then cook them. We ate those rabbits. They were delicious.

Despite the dire circumstances at home, the foundation for Christian values was there. Like discipline. I think I was fortunate that my grandmother and mother were strict, no-nonsense, religious folks. You followed God's law, no matter what, and you knew how to behave. I took on those values. I knew not to steal and not to use bad language. I got in trouble once for saying "son of a gun." I bought into all of it. I didn't care what anybody thought, if it wasn't along the lines of what we were taught with spirituality with the Bible and Sunday school and that sort of thing. I pretty much wasn't going to be influenced by anything said outside of that.

We never missed church or Sunday school. I loved going. That's the only place we did go except for outside to play.

We'd walk to church, because we didn't have a car until I graduated from high school. We dressed for church. For me, that meant the same set of clothes every time we went. Of course, my mother would iron whatever we had, our suit or pants.

Church lasted most of the day. I miss that. I enjoyed that so much. We would have a Sunday school service in the morning, then church for an hour or two. Maybe we'd have a snack after that, or we'd go home and then go back to the evening service. Later, when we became Pentecostal, the services were a lot longer.

The African Methodist Episcopal church is where we belonged. AME churches aren't really that spirited. On the other hand, Pentecostal is really spirited, complete with dancing and tambourines. Sometimes we'd visit other churches, too. Most of the churches were well attended.

Daddy Walt never went with us to church. But when he got drunk, he'd talk about God. He'd say, "God is love. God is love."

My mother went to Alabama State, which was a "normal" school. My stepmother also went to Alabama State. Normal schools were created to train high school graduates to be teachers. Now they are just called "teachers colleges." The idea was you would go to this school to become a teacher to help your people.

I don't know how much my mother's education helped her in the job market. I do know she worked as a dispatcher for a cab company in 1955, which plunked her down right in the middle of a significant moment in history.

On December 1, 1955, Rosa Parks, a 43-year-old seamstress, refused to follow the order of a bus driver to surrender her seat in the "colored section" of the bus to a White passenger. She got arrested for civil disobedience in violation of Alabama segregation laws. At the time, approximately seven of ten people riding the bus were Black, and they had to follow the prevailing regulations. Seats at the front of the bus were for White passengers, seats at the rear of the bus were for Black passengers, and the center portion of the bus was contingent on a floating color line that could move in either direction depending on the composition of the passengers. If more White passengers got on the bus and there weren't available seats in the middle, the bus driver was obliged to make a Black passenger surrender his or her seat.

After Parks's arrest, Black leaders called for a boycott of the bus companies. But this left Black workers in a lurch for finding transportation to get to work. Montgomery had 18 Black-owned taxi companies at the time, and they helped by agreeing to charge passengers just ten cents a ride—the same price as bus fare—on the day of the boycott. My mother was right in the middle of all of that, trying to get people taxis. She actually talked to Martin Luther King and Ralph Abernathy.

Dr. King made a speech, where he told a gathering:

*There comes a time when people get tired. We are here this evening to say to those who have mistreated us so long that we are tired—tired of being segregated and humiliated, tired of being kicked about by the brutal feet of oppression. . . . We had no alternative but to protest.*

*If you will protest courageously, and yet with dignity . . . when the history books are written in future generations, the historians will have to pause and say, "There lived a great people – a Black people – who injected new meaning and dignity into the veins of civilization."*

That boycott lasted until November 13, 1956, when the U.S. Supreme Court ruled that segregation on Montgomery's buses was unconstitutional. After the change was made, Rosa Parks became one of the first to ride the buses. According to a December 31, 1956, *Time* magazine article, "she gazed peacefully out a bus window from a seat of her own choosing."

My stepfather got transferred to Murfreesboro, Tennessee, after I finished first grade. Notice I said "finished" and not "passed"? That's because I failed first grade. Who fails first grade, right?

Well, I had a strict teacher at Loveless Elementary School. And I think the reason I failed had more to do with something I did than my performance in the classroom.

I threw some tissue paper on the floor when my teacher was sweeping. I wasn't mad at her or anything, I was just thinking, "She's sweeping anyway, so I'll put this on the floor." Boy, did that make her mad. To me it was just logic. I've always got in a lot of trouble for that kind of thinking. I still think like that on way too many things. Eventually, I figured, "That's why I got held back." That or the fact I'd talked back too much, which I've always done. Either way, a promise of a better life was awaiting us approximately 300 miles away in Murfreesboro, Tennessee, where my stepfather got transferred. For me, things would be a little more familiar since I had to repeat the first grade.

# CHAPTER TWO

Being hungry is something I don't wish on anyone.

We moved to Murfreesboro, Tennessee, when Daddy Walt got transferred to Sewart Air Force Base, which is located 12 miles southeast of Murfreesboro, a city located smack in the middle of the anvil-shaped state. Originally, the place was named "Cannonsburgh" for Newton Cannon, a member of the state legislature. Later, they adopted the name "Murfreesboro" for Revolutionary War hero Colonel Hardy Murfree. Those insignificant facts about Murfreesboro do not concern me. Murfreesboro to me represented a different way of life. After we lived there a while, the realization came to me that we were dirt poor and that food was scarce. I also understood for the first time that I wanted to help the plight of Black children; this desire helped pave my path to NABSE.

I'm not sure if being "hungry" is the right way to describe our situation in Tennessee. More accurate would be we were anxious for food. We got to eat, but it was like, "Am I going to get enough?"

Typically, we'd have grits for breakfast. For lunch, we'd take to school a hard-boiled egg. Sometimes we'd take a sandwich—usually a peanut butter sandwich.

We had chicken for dinner, a lot. At those meals, the question would be whether you'd get a choice piece or not. Poor people know about choice pieces. They are a regular, nice-sized piece of chicken, like a breast, or even a leg. But an unchoice piece would be a back—not much meat. You might get a choice and a back, and you might get a choice and a wing. But sometimes you get a choice only. You'd have that, then you'd maybe have some green beans or a small portion of mashed potatoes, maybe a piece of light bread.

For your drink on a good day, you would have water and sugar. On a better day, you would have a half a glass of Kool-Aid. But whether it was Kool-Aid or water and sugar, it was only half a glass because there wasn't enough for four or five of us. We religiously played the promotional games by Pepsi Cola, and Coke, where you would keep track of their coupons, and if you got real lucky you would be awarded a case of Coke. For the most part, I realized that we were not doing well. We were struggling. And whatever you were served on any given day would determine whether your stomach continued to growl or not.

While we didn't have a lot of food, everything we ate was fresh. I still look for some of the tastes I had back then. We were eating organic long before eating organic became cool.

In general, living in Murfreesboro felt like a step down from Montgomery, where we had family and knew a lot of people. They often helped feed us, so we never worried about eating. I had an aunt in Montgomery who had a horizontal freezer—we'd never heard of such a thing where someone had a freezer stuffed with food. We also had our own house in Montgomery, but in Murfreesboro we lived in a project. Tennessee just wasn't as good in our minds.

I went from first grade through the fourth while in Murfreesboro. Yes, I passed the first grade my second time around. Somewhere during that time, the school system acquired the free lunch program. Boy, did that ever make me happy.

At the time, I didn't think about the anxiety I endured worrying about whether I would be hungry or not. Later it came to me that I never wanted to experience that again.

Christmas brought a lot of anxiety, too. I can't tell you how many Christmas Eves I sat and wondered whether Santa Claus would visit or not.

We would take trips from Murfreesboro to Detroit in the summer to see my real father. And we'd occasionally go back to Montgomery. My sister and I took a bus trip without any adults to Montgomery on one occasion. That trip would make a profound impact on my life.

Since my sister, Birdie seven, and me were nine years old, the plan called for the bus driver to watch us. When we got to Birmingham, we were still sitting at the front of the bus when the driver told us, "You two need to go on back and make room for people coming in."

That made sense to me. People were coming onto the bus, and we needed to make room for them. That seemed like the polite thing to do. Accordingly, Birdie and I moved about halfway back. No cause for alarm, right?

People continued to board the bus, and a few moments later, the bus driver again addressed us. This time his voice sounded gruff and threatening: "Didn't I tell you two to get back there? Now get in the back!" We're like, "Okay, we'll go to the back."

Based on the kind of home life I had—and the fact somebody always seemed to be upset with me—I didn't attribute the treatment to us being Black. I related it to us not following their directions. Once we finally walked all the way to the back, we found two Black kids sitting there, a boy and a girl. They were younger than we were, and they were petrified. Keep in mind, I was nine years old and Birdie was seven. I saw myself in them. And I thought, "How awful it was that somebody would do that to little people." Even though I was just a kid, I knew what they were doing on that bus was wrong and shouldn't have been happening. Then I got sad. Why would you do that to little people? Even to this day, the injustice of it all chokes me up. I've seen other sad things in my life since then, but that one

I've never been able to erase from my memory. How could anybody do that to any person?

That's the first time I thought about helping other people. I've always been emotional about people not doing people right ever since. I told myself that going forward if I could ever help somebody, I would do so. NABSE preached the need to reach every child and that not everyone had every child's interest at heart. That incident on the bus served up my first exposure to discrimination, too.

Having no self-esteem, I would have done anything to feel special, even for just a moment. That moment finally occurred, because I could run fast.

May Day in Murfreesboro brought an annual celebration of the spring and the coming summer. May Day festivities always took place on May 1. For the kids of Murfreesboro, the celebration meant all kinds of competitions, even for youngsters my age. Included among those activities was a running race.

I'd just finished first grade when I attended May Day for the first time. The race for those my age was 25 yards in distance and it took place in a flat field behind the school. They marked an area covered by dirt and grass with running lanes, but it certainly wasn't a track. Of course, I ran barefoot because I basically went barefoot everywhere, as did all the other kids in Murfreesboro.

We lined up. There were eight to ten kids in the race. They didn't have a starter's pistol, rather they went with "On your mark. Get set. Go!" I took off, and left everybody else in the dust, winning easily. That victory brought me my first ribbon along with an awareness, like, "Looks as though I'm pretty fast."

I went into the next year's race knowing that I was faster than everybody else. Since I was always a thoughtful kid and overly polite, I let the other kids get off to a fast start before I got going. I still beat them and won another ribbon.

In the race that took place after I finished third grade, I got off to a fast start and somebody tripped me. I sprang to my feet, and, somehow, I still managed to win.

My final May Day race came after fourth grade. Prior to that one, I said to myself, "I'm not taking any chances, I'm going to take off and get out to a big lead before anybody can trick me or mess me up." My earlier success in the previous races told me I would win the race. Sure enough, I bolted way out in front of everybody at the start. I figured I'd taken care of any possible dirty tricks until I approached the finish line, and I'm like, "I'll be darned, they've come up with another trick."

At least that's what I thought.

They'd run a string across the track. I didn't know the idea was to be the first runner to break through the string. I'd never seen string at the finish line. I thought this was some obstacle or hazard. What was I supposed to do? The answer came instinctively. I jumped over the string like I was clearing a hurdle.

Winning fascinated me. I'd never won anything in my life, and I didn't really feel like I was good at anything, then suddenly it's like, "My goodness. I'm fast. I can beat these guys."

I had no idea where being fast could take me. Suffice it to say, being fast served me a massive dose of positive feelings, and you would have thought such a positive feeling would spill over to home. Daddy Walt and my mother were hardly impressed. Not the slightest acknowledgement of what I'd accomplished.

Fact is, back then I never had any discussions with the adults other than them telling me, "Don't do this, don't do that, and clean this or that."

While I didn't receive any praise for my triumphs because I was a child, that didn't keep me from doing work normally reserved for the adults. Because I was the oldest, I did a lot of child care. That would continue through high school. I probably changed the diapers of all my siblings, save for Birdie. I just knew I had to do it when my mother and stepfather weren't there. That was a lot for a kid to do. In later years, I would discover that my siblings really looked up to me. They remembered me being in their corner, even spanking them at times. And they were grateful. I found that quite touching.

The work I had to do helping to take care of the other kids in the family probably fueled my feelings of protest when my mother announced she was pregnant with my final sibling.

Birdie is my sister from my mother and my real father. And there was a sister before her who died in childbirth. My mother had several children die in childbirth. After that came Michael O'Neal, my stepfather's first son with my mother, then Annette O'Neal and Antonio O'Neal, and finally, Edward O'Neal. When my mother was pregnant with Edward, I remember asking her why she was having another kid. I pointed out we barely had enough food to go around among us. I hated that she was pregnant. I was mad at my mother, and I wanted to be mad at my brother. Like I told her, we didn't have enough food at the time, and we didn't have enough room, so I'm like, "What are you doing having another?" To this day, my mother talks about my reaction to her being pregnant with my youngest brother.

Living in the project in Murfreesboro, had a weird and different vibe—that and not having any family there. Just like Alabama, only

Blacks lived in our Murfreesboro neighborhood. Of course, I didn't think of it being Black or White, either way.

Murfreesboro marked the first time I tried a cigarette. A Winston. That happened in the third or fourth grade when I was hanging out with friends. Like most kids who try a cigarette for the first time, I thought it was daring and cool. Thank goodness I didn't like it. I never tried smoking again. And I learned how to ride a bicycle in Murfreesboro after getting a bicycle for Christmas. Nobody taught me. I practiced on a small sidewalk on a hill in the projects until I finally got it down. Learning to ride a bike is a big accomplishment for any kid. Doing so made me feel like I owned the world, because I gained a certain amount of independence by being able to ride to places farther away. Riding a bike helped to build up my legs, too. At that age, I wasn't consciously trying to build up my leg muscles, but it helped. Ultimately, I think that helped to contribute to how fast a runner I would become.

My home life still didn't provide any semblance of a role model. Daddy Walt just didn't fit the bill. That area continued to remain lacking. However, when I reached the fourth grade, I got my first role model and my first job when I went to work for a retired dentist. I don't remember his name. I do remember that he was a kind old man who treated me nice and that he had worn and wrinkled black skin.

He'd set up a general store of sorts in a tiny, one-car garage. I guess he must have asked my mother if I could run his store, because she allowed me to go to his place after school and on the weekends to work behind the counter selling canned goods, Coca-Cola, candy, popcorn, you name it. I liked the job. He paid me 50 cents a week. I looked forward to going over there, which might have been because of the patience he showed me. That meant everything. Like taking the time to demonstrate how to sweep. I'd never swept before, so I didn't know the proper technique with a broom. I tried to sweep the long way, all the way down the sidewalk instead of back and forth.

Neither my stepfather nor my real father were around and neither seemed to care about me, yet, for some reason, this man did. He'd be inside his house while I worked in the garage and people came by to buy things.

I would sell the stuff and leave the money for him. Having that job was refreshing. Gave me a feeling of freedom. I remember being at his house thinking how nice it was.

Another memorable moment from Tennessee came in the form of a beating. We're talking a good old-fashioned beating. The kind of beating parents don't do these days.

Everybody my age will tell you about a time when they were growing up and one of their parents told them to go get a stick from off the tree that they could beat you with. Here's what happened.

I kind of had a thing for heroes. Like my hero from the Bible was Samson. When we switched from the Methodist to Baptist church in Tennessee, I'd wear a hat and tell everyone the hat was my hair and that I needed my hair all the time or I'd lose my strength.

Popeye was another of my heroes. I wanted to be like Popeye. I watched *Popeye the Sailor* on our black-and-white TV, which we didn't have when we were in Alabama. Because I wanted to be like Popeye, I wanted to eat spinach, and that's where the problem originated.

I stole money out of my mother's purse to buy spinach. Imagine a kid stealing money to buy spinach. Remember, my mother was all about the Bible. "Thou shalt not steal" ranked prominently among the commandments. Thus, my mother deemed stealing punishable with a whipping. Well, I got caught, so she beat me, and then made me eat the spinach. I hated it, of course.

After the fourth grade, we moved again.

Daddy Walt completed his enlistment and we returned to Montgomery, where we lived with Daddy Walt's mother for the summer. Those were stressful days.

34

One time we were swimming nude at a pond in Montgomery and we saw a snake in the water. Daddy Walt came and got me. For whatever reason, I got a good beating for that. He told me, "Don't you ever do that again."

Another time I'd gone to the local theater to see *Cleopatra* starring Elizabeth Taylor and Richard Burton. I just loved the movies. Still do. And I couldn't wait to see this one. But Daddy Walt came into the movie house and dragged me out. That made me so mad. I never did see the full movie. He explained that he did what he did because I hadn't asked him for permission to go.

I hate to use the word hate. But my being around Daddy Walt was pretty darn close to hate.

While we were there that summer, Daddy Walt's mother told him that living in Alabama wasn't the place for him and his family, so he re-enlisted in the Air Force and we moved again.

Moving wasn't something we dreaded. We considered moving an adventure, because we never got to go anywhere. Goldsboro, North Carolina, turned out to be our new landing spot.

# CHAPTER THREE

Fifth grade at Greenleaf Elementary in Goldsboro, North Carolina, became a significant point in my life because I experienced my first male teacher. Each of my teachers from first through fourth grades had been a woman. So here I had my first male teacher, and he turned out to be special for several reasons.

His classroom ran smoothly, really organized. And he was strict. Not in a bad way, but from the point of view that he had certain standards and he insisted we were all going to do well in this class because we're all going to do A-B-C-D-E-F-G, whatever it was, and we were going to do those things the right way.

Most impressive to me was how he made everybody remember the Gettysburg Address and give a speech about it. Later in my life, I'd wonder why the practice of memorizing things ceased. I considered memorization an exercise that was particularly effective.

Thus, I learned the Gettysburg Address. I can't tell you how proud I was to be able to recite the whole thing by memory. All the practice I did to get ready to do that made learning Abraham Lincoln's memorable speech an accomplishment.

This teacher taught all subjects effectively. For the first time in my life, learning really excited me. I wanted to learn more.

I derived a lot of satisfaction having this man as my teacher. Through him, I gained my first real study discipline and motivation for striving to have high-quality outcomes for myself in terms of achievement. He'd be like, "You can do this, you just have to work on it."

Like any top-notch teacher, he did more than just teach. And he showed an immeasurable amount of kindness to me.

I had problems with wetting the bed. Yes, I was in the fifth grade, but it was just something I couldn't control. Even when we were in Detroit, I wet the bed. I felt bad because my stepmother already didn't like the fact that we were there. She got used to it because she couldn't do anything about it. Had I gone to a therapist he probably would have surmised that my homelife contributed to why I wet the bed. Still, wetting the bed is difficult for any child to endure, particularly if you were in the fifth grade.

Wetting in the bed leaves an undeniable stench. Well, this teacher that I admired so further demonstrated why I still consider him to have been so special. One day, he obviously caught a whiff of the way I smelled. Rather than address me in front of my classmates, he discreetly took me aside and told me I needed to shower before school because I didn't want to be smelling in the classroom. The tender way in which he handled that discussion showed a true compassionate side.

Greenleaf Elementary School's principal had a reputation for swatting kids. And he had a thing about kids who didn't clean their plates at lunch. If you didn't finish what you ate, you had a choice of rethinking that position, or he would smack you. So everybody knew that if you weren't going to eat something, you had better stuff the food into an empty milk carton to avoid facing the principal's wrath.

Well, I hated coleslaw. Coleslaw has mayonnaise in it, and I'd stayed away from mayonnaise ever since my mother married Daddy Walt. Trying to chug mayonnaise like a milkshake will do that to a kid. That didn't result in a good outcome back then, and I didn't have a good outcome at Greenleaf with the coleslaw, either. Normally, I would have jammed the coleslaw into the milk carton right away to make sure I didn't have to eat it. But this one day, I was talking a bunch—I've always talked a lot, and I'm just chatting away. I forgot to stuff my food into the milk carton and get the heck out of the lunchroom. The principal caught me. Since I didn't want to get beat, I ate that slaw, then I puked all the way back to class.

To this day, I still don't eat mayonnaise or anything with mayonnaise in it.

38

Goldsboro brought me my first experience with the Ku Klux Klan when I went to a movie with some friends my age.

The theater was segregated, which, as I mentioned before, didn't really mean anything to me. I mean, there were "colored only" water fountains, too. "Colored people" could only sit in the balcony at the theater. That seemed odd because I felt like the balcony seats were better than those below. I don't remember what movie we saw that day, but when we left the theater and began walking home one of the guys I was with blurted out, "Look over there, those guys have sheets on."

I didn't understand what the Ku Klux Klan was. I just knew there were four or five of them standing outside in the middle of the afternoon. I thought, "Well, they sure look funny." Then they started walking toward us with a sense of urgency and we felt threatened. We were like, "They're coming after us, we better get the heck out of here." So we ran like fools to get away. Even though grown men were wearing those sheets and I was only in the fifth grade, I was fast enough to get away from them. We didn't get caught. After all, they were running in sheets.

I started noticing girls before we moved to Goldsboro, and almost kissed one when I found myself in a school clothes rack in Murfreesboro. But I was too shy or scared, and I ended up playfully slapping her instead. In Goldsboro, I had a little girlfriend, Dee-Dee.

She was cute, and she became the first girl I ever kissed. Getting that first kiss made me feel special, and awkward. For some reason I got the feeling she was coming on to me. I even told her I did not believe in sex before marriage. To this day, I still don't have the slightest idea about why I felt the need to say that. I didn't know anything about sex. We talked about it when we were little boys in Alabama. And I remember spying on a babysitter lying down with a boy who came to visit her. But basically, I didn't have a clue about sex.

While in Goldsboro, I began to have a deeper understanding of the Christian faith. A big part of my faith was driven by what I'd seen on that bus that day a few years earlier.

A lot of times I'll get asked when I got saved. I can't exactly remember what the preacher was saying when it happened, or the date or time, but it hit me, "This is what I believe." And I know that is the moment I accepted Christ.

Everything felt right about accepting Jesus Christ into my life. The biggest thing that resonated with me then, and still does, was that love overcomes everything. Christ loved folks despite any shortcomings or faults they may have. That's why I've always tried to accept everyone. It doesn't matter who you are, or why you are, everybody has their reason for being the way they are. Christ loves everybody no matter what. That's kind of been my motto.

Ironically, as much as Daddy Walt's abusive ways ran counter to a stereotypical Christian's, he didn't have a problem with me accepting Christ. He didn't think I was some kind of sissy for doing so.

Daddy Walt believed in God. He didn't believe in being a sissy though. Because he always said you better fight back. But he would want to preach late at night when he got drunk. This started when I'd be up when he got back from the bars. He'd say, "You don't even know what God means, boy. You don't even know what God means. God means love."

While I agreed with his message, I didn't really feel those words coming from him. Daddy Walt's sermons from the kitchen always perplexed me.

Other than that, Daddy Walt never really talked to me much about anything. But sometimes when he'd come in late at night, he'd cook these amazing stews. He just had a knack for cooking stew. Because I'd stay up late most nights studying, I'd still be up. And I was always hungry. His stews were like soups. A lot of ketchup. Maybe some hot sauce, neck bones, which are great. Rice. If he had chicken, chicken. Peas, and all kinds of vegetables. He'd say, "I'm going to see how much you can eat," and would sure get a kick out of it. I always ate whatever he made. He couldn't fix enough.

The one year in Goldsboro led to another assignment change for Daddy Walt—we were heading to Nellis Air Force Base in Las Vegas.

Moving to Las Vegas filled us with excitement. We'd heard all kinds of things about California, like during the black-and-white cartoons we watched on TV where the characters were like, "We're going to California, boy oh boy!" We didn't know Las Vegas was in Nevada and not California. We'd never heard of the state of Nevada. Then we went out there and saw that desert.

I remember the train ride to Nevada because I got sick as a dog, which I think was motion sickness. When we arrived, we continued to be excited about the new adventure. Traveling still gives me hope for what's to come. It's always been an adventure, and I embraced it early on.

That summer we lived in a housing project called Cadillac Arms near Kit Carson Elementary. We were scared about going there since we heard it was a rough school. The place we lived in didn't have air conditioning. I don't know whether the building came without it or it simply didn't work. It didn't matter. I do know the conditions were miserable. The kids slept on the floor and we sweated a lot. Thank goodness we moved at the end of the summer to a residence on Gold Street near Matt Kelly Elementary School, a school that was segregated like the South. So, it was similar to

Goldsboro, North Carolina, Tennessee, and Alabama—all
segregated. I became a safety patrol in sixth grade at Matt Kelly.
Being on duty helped alert me to the fact I was a wimp. I didn't get
beat up, but some guys wanted to beat me up. One of them threw a
rock that caught me on my head—split the skin wide open. When I
got home and Daddy Walt saw my head, he asked what happened. I
told him the truth and he gave me a whipping for not fighting back.
That episode set the tumblers of my mind to working. I knew I
wanted to learn how to defend myself. I told myself if I ever had the
chance to learn how to defend myself I would make the most of it.
(Our family left the house near Matt Kelly in the middle of the
school year, so I was still in the sixth grade.)

During the middle of the year in sixth grade, we moved to
Henderson, Nevada. Back then it was a dump, but it is now a
gorgeous suburb of Las Vegas. I went to Seward Elementary, my
first integrated school. I really didn't have any experience with
ongoing racism in school at that point of my life. I mean, I
experienced the KKK in Goldsboro, but I didn't really feel
threatened, even though I ran. I thought those guys were clowns. I
didn't think about somebody discriminating against me because of
my skin color in Nevada. But in Henderson, there was this one time
that I was made to feel conspicuous because of my skin color.

At school, they asked me to help sell popsicles during recess. They set up the front of a room where they stored the lawn equipment. There were three of us. One of the girls was White. And I thought she was cute. We stood together behind a little table. For some reason, somebody turned the lights out, and this White girl said, "I can't see you, Bernard." That's when I first realized I was different. I'm like, *"They think I'm Black."* Her comment didn't sit well. That was the first time from all our moving around that I remember being made to feel different.

My sixth-grade teacher in Henderson, Mr. Douglas, who later became a principal, was the first White teacher I ever had in school, and he really encouraged me. I'd occasionally go to his house and I enjoyed having his company. Being around a role model, who also was a man, meant a lot to me. He used to race me, too. That led to me becoming the first sixth grader to ever beat him in a race.

Away from school I started selling *Grit* newspaper door to door for 50 cents in Henderson. I kept getting rejected for a regular paper route. I didn't own a bicycle, so they didn't think I could do it. I continued to be persistent, going to the newspaper guy every other week until he gave me a job. I told him I could walk and run fast to deliver papers. So I got a real paper job in sixth grade. I had to be up at 4:30 a.m. to fold papers and walk the route.

Fifth grade and sixth grade hold a special place in my memories because of the role models I had.

I advanced to junior high—I first attended Henderson Junior High and then Jim Bridger Junior High. We moved from Henderson to Nellis Air Base in Las Vegas, where I was zoned for Jim Bridger Junior High. I'd ride the bus home from Jim Bridger. One day we saw where a jet had crashed in our neighborhood. We weren't witness to the actual crash, but the crash site of that F-15 was still fresh when we passed by. Seeing the devastation and destruction of that crash seemed to impact all of us. Somebody obviously had died in the crash, so that made me sad. Most of the kids I rode the bus with were Air Force kids. I knew they were thinking it could have been their father or someone they knew piloting that plane. Many Armed Forces brats had things in common. The site of that crash reminded us of the service our families gave to our country. I realized then how much patriotism I had for our country. Another positive experience from being in Daddy Walt's family.

Everybody says how they remember where they were when JFK got shot. For me, I was at Jim Bridger Junior High. That made me sad, too. I'm not sure anybody knew how to act when the president got assassinated.

After the eighth grade, Daddy Walt got transferred again. This time Okinawa became our destination.

CHAPTER FOUR

Going to Okinawa proved to be a good move for me, even though I liked Las Vegas. We lived there during my ninth and tenth grade years of school.

I took up judo in Okinawa, and I learned to be good at it. I loved the definition of judo as a gentle sport, since as a Christian, deflecting hits and kicks was not aggressive but kind. I had a lot of other life experiences in Japan, too. I saw my first Shakespearean play, and loved it. I learned how to type. And I became aware that quality teaching could make a difference in my education.

Okinawa's location had ensured that it would be right in the middle of things when the invading Allied forces arrived during World War II. That resulted in the Battle of Okinawa, which lasted approximately three months and wiped out many civilians. An American presence was still prevalent at Okinawa when we were there.

Daddy Walt was stationed at Kadena Air Base and we lived on the main island of Okinawa. Due to Daddy Walt's low rank, we never did get base housing in Okinawa. We stayed in the village, right in the middle of where the Okinawans lived. Daddy Walt's behavior—even overseas—continued. Every time anything went right for him, like getting a promotion, he'd do something stupid and get busted back to his previous rank. Usually that involved him having too much to drink and getting into a fight. If I didn't know better, I would have thought that he just didn't want to hold a higher rank.

We lived in two places while in Okinawa. At that first place we lived, I experienced an unexpected occurrence that caused more than a little bit of excitement.

While studying late—maybe 1 o'clock or 2 o'clock in the morning, I suddenly felt shaking all around me. The house felt like it might come apart. That's when I thought, "Well, it looks like God is talking to us." I couldn't figure out what in the world was happening. Then it stopped. I realized I'd just survived my first earthquake.

Living in Okinawa, we had a better quality of life. Those Japanese were poorer than we were. We even had paid service, something we never had in the United States. We paid somebody to cut the grass and they didn't even use a lawn mower. They used hand sickles. And boy, were they fast. They'd get after that grass and they'd be done in no time. Then they'd come into the house and take a break to eat rice. They fascinated me with how they could eat that rice with their chopsticks. I ended up loving rice. Probably watching those guys with their chopsticks had a lot to do with that.

The second place we lived had a closer proximity to the base. I could either walk to the base or take the bus to get there. Mind you, all these buses were Japanese, so you needed to have a plan about where you wanted to get off. That convenience allowed me to start hanging out at the base after school. Being able to hang out after school paved the way for me to start taking judo.

I attended Kubasaki High School, which was, and still is, a United States Department of Defense Dependents School on Okinawa. Today it's the second oldest operating high school in the Department of Defense Dependents Schools system.

Kubasaki was located on Naha Air Base, which was built in 1933, and known as Oroku Naval Air Base. Eventually, the United States captured the base in World War II by way of the Battle of Okinawa. After the war, the United States stationed themselves there in an effort to maintain control of the Pacific. The Naha Air Base eventually was operated for military as well as civilian air travel between Tokyo and Okinawa.

I'm not exactly sure when the lights went on for me as far as being obsessed with education and getting smarter. I'd started studying hard in the sixth grade when we lived in Las Vegas. I would get on my knees every night and beg God to please let me make good grades, so I could do well in junior high, because I wanted to do well in high school. I did not feel I was smart enough for college but thought if I worked hard enough and continued praying, God might answer my prayers if I was persistent asking. Maybe that stemmed from my low self-esteem. I just never thought I could do the work to get into college, and I didn't think I'd be able to pay for it even if I was able to get into college.

A counselor at Kubasaki had a profound effect on me. I credit her with sending another miracle my way. She told me, "I know your grades aren't that great, but you need to really work hard. If you get really good grades, you can get a scholarship and go to college." Her words inspired me to no end. I felt like I could fly to the moon. That counselor got me so motivated, I said, "Maybe I can get to college." That made me study even more. I continued to pray equally hard every night. I don't know what hit me, or whatever, but I know that my nightly prayers for doing well in school were meant to accomplish one big goal: to escape our current way of life.

The teachers at Kubasaki were strict. They established high standards, and we always had a lot of homework. When they said military school, they meant it. You had to work.

The teachers weren't in the military. They were private citizens. They were regular teachers, who had to apply to become an armed services teacher. They got paid well, and they got nice packages to become one of those teachers. The military tried to hire the best, and as I'd find out once we returned to the United States, their work with me and my classmates paid off.

Despite the counselor's positive words to me about me going to college, I struggled with my grades at Kubasaki. Those struggles led me to seek help. I learned that other students could help me study. That awareness prompted me to seek friends who could help me in the classroom. Many of those classmates I befriended were colonels' sons and grew up under far better circumstances than myself. I certainly felt thankful that they would help me with my studies.

Getting that help opened my eyes to what I lacked culturally in my upbringing at home. I could see that these other kids were surrounded by culture. They had parents who didn't drink excessively. Everyone in their family read books. They lived in much nicer houses than we ever could imagine. They wore much nicer clothes. They had fine silverware and other trappings familiar to wealthy families. And the dinners they served at their houses were like nothing I'd seen. One time I got teased at one of those dinners for having my pinky out when I ate. I thought my attempt at proper was fancy, when basically, I knew nothing about table manners. I also noticed that these friends of mine worked hard at their studies.

Seeing how the other half lived prompted me to think: "Daddy Walt, can you please just get a promotion already?"

My first Shakespearean play was a high school production of *Julius Caesar*—"Et tu, Brute?" I loved it. From then on, I was hooked. When I later studied Shakespeare in high school back in the United States, I took right to it. Why was I so attracted to Shakespeare? I think it stemmed from a desire to be more culturally advanced. That formal talk mesmerized me. I always was impressed by things that you needed to have a higher intellect to appreciate.

A colonel's son, Jerry, became my best friend in Okinawa. He and his family were from Connecticut. I told Jerry how everyone would make fun of my Southern accent every time I went to visit my father in Detroit. Jerry helped me change my accent. I just copied the way the Connecticut boy talked. Eventually, when we went back to Vegas, people would say, "You talk funny." I had that adopted accent from Jerry. I left my Southern accent in Okinawa.

Shedding some previous personal traits allowed me to pick up new ones, like self-defense skills through judo. One thing I learned really quickly while living in Japan was that I needed to get tougher. Someone told me they taught judo classes in the gym at the military base.

A tough Black guy taught the class. Oh man, nobody would have mistaken him for anything other than a badass. I don't know if he'd seen combat during his military career, but I would have been surprised to find out he had not. The guy had been cast in concrete. I couldn't help but be impressed by how well this guy was put together, particularly since I was a skinny nothing.

The instructor ran the class like it was Japanese. He adhered to all the traditional judo teachings, which made the gym a "dojo." Following suit, the instructor was known as "Sensei"—which is what we called him. The gym wasn't fancy, and consisted of four walls and padded mats.

Judo originated to provide a means for defending yourself with your body serving as your only weapon. You want to pin an opponent to the ground or force him to surrender by applying a chokehold or joint lock. You can strike, thrust, or use weapons defense to throw an opponent or take him down. You are defending yourself with nothing but your own body.

Ironically, as big of a wimp as I was, judo came easy to me.

Part of that ease stemmed from my athleticism. I didn't really think about being athletic, but from all my years of running and riding a bicycle, the muscles in my legs were powerful.

The first day of class, the instructor had us lie down and practice slapping the mat. Seemed like that must have lasted 20 or 30 minutes. You're lying down, and you bring your hands up and slap the mat. Then you'd squat, and you'd fall back, and slap the mat. Then you'd go from a squat until you stood. You just kept doing all of that.

I attended judo practice religiously. I learned how to flip and fall and I advanced to where I knew how to do the foot sweeps and the throws. After we did our drills we would spar with the other students. Sparring is known as "randori" in judo vernacular.

A popular judo saying is that the best defense is to walk or run away from physical conflict. I found that to be true in my pursuit to learn judo and the confidence that it instilled.

Randori with the other students eventually led to randori with the Sensei, though he wouldn't randori with everyone. The first time he picked me, I couldn't believe it.

Sensei had an amazing ability to foot sweep an opponent, primarily because of his technique. He could execute all the moves flawlessly, and he moved fast.

We bowed prior to starting my first randori with the instructor. Seconds later, I found myself on my back. I hadn't even had time to think about moving my foot forward or to the left. He foot swept me

53

over and over. I'd move around some more, and boom, I was on the ground. Twenty or 30 times he did that. That wasn't easy to endure. He wasn't picking on me. I got the same treatment from him that he gave everyone else the first time he went to the mat with them. Through that instruction, I became an incredible foot sweeper. That became my signature move. I mastered the technique, and my natural athletic ability revealed itself in the speed with which I executed the foot sweep. I also got good at flipping my opponent over my back.

I competed in the 145- and 154-pound weight classes. Usually my matches lasted less than five to ten seconds. I would bow, then I'd foot sweep my opponent as soon as they touched me. After that, they would be on their back. Since my matches ended so quickly, I'd be relaxing, drinking juice, and watching everybody else finish their matches. There was nothing to it. I would do just like Sensei.

Like I said, judo just came to me easily.

Sensei taught that you only needed to defend yourself. You deflect. So that was part of my Christian belief—don't hurt anyone. The translation of judo is "gentle way." I was taught that if you tried to resist against a more powerful opponent, you would get defeated. However, if you adjusted, and dodged the attack by your opponent, you could cause him to get off balance. That reduced his power, so no matter his size, you could defeat him. So basically, a weaker opponent is not necessarily going to get beat up.

Since judo was born in Japan, the best way to improve your technique was to go up against Japanese natives. Sensei understood the Japanese culture. From that came his insistence that to advance from one belt to the next, you couldn't compete at the gym. You had to go to the village. We were directed where to go. Accordingly, we would take the bus to one of the Japanese villages, find the dojo, smile, and bow to the master. I would give him my name and fight against the Japanese.

The sensei knew we were coming there to compete. If you could compete against a Japanese national, you were just going to get that much better because you had to know what you were doing if you wanted to have any chance of not getting humiliated. A lot of them were short, but there were some who were my height and weight. Some were a little chubby. Still, going there for the first time was intimidating. These guys were about as accomplished as you could be in judo. But I felt confident. And I won, over and over, earning my advancements. That's how I got moved from white, to green, to brown belt. That boosted my confidence like nobody's business.

I did everything the Japanese did. When they waited for the bus, they would squat. I'd squat, too, because there were no chairs.

They'd just look at me and smile. I just got a kick out of the Japanese environment.

Continuing to advance while going up against the students at Japanese dojo really built my confidence. I felt pretty good about myself. I knew that in the future, if anybody tried something, I could take care of myself. My confidence was so great, nobody ever bothered me. I don't know if I was just a confident Black man, or just good at judo. I never was intimidated by anyone after that, no matter how tall they were, skinny, fat, or big. Nobody dared to throw rocks at me again.

Sensei overly emphasized stretching, telling us we needed to stretch all the time no matter where we were. To this day, I still stretch a lot. I can still touch both hands to the floor without bending my knees, and I can almost do a full split. Later, stretching would help me when I started running track.

Most afternoons after practicing judo, I'd go to the recreation center to find Jerry. We'd spend the rest of the afternoon shooting pool. That rec center had all the bells and whistles. Armed services took care of their people pretty well. We went to dances there sometime, too. There were several rooms and all of them were well kept. I got good at pool, too, but not as good as I got in judo. I did enjoy shooting pool, though.

I liked Jerry's sister, and had a little crush on her. I didn't date her. I just admired her. I had no idea at that time about the stigma of a Black man and a White woman. Not in the least. No idea. I do know that Jerry's parents didn't have a problem with me coming over to their house to study, eat dinner, or anything like that.

We moved back to the United States after my sophomore year in high school, returning to Las Vegas.

I liked Japan quite a bit, but my brothers and sisters and I longed for home while we were there. I think if we would have stayed in Okinawa a little longer, I might have developed a relationship with Jerry's sister. I missed the chance with her because I was too chicken to ask her out and I didn't want to risk losing a great friend in Jerry.

There were some cons to living in Japan that I would not miss when we left. The prevalence of lizards creeped me out the whole time we lived in Okinawa. I'd hear them on the roof and they ran around everywhere. They were called Ryukyu japalure, and they were big, like iguanas. I also didn't like the fact that on Okinawa you were restricted. You were isolated on an island, and you saw the same stuff over and over.

Okinawa had been great, but we were all happy to be returning to the United States.

# CHAPTER FIVE

We returned to the United States, and Las Vegas, before my junior year in high school. And I arrived with renewed hope about going to college.

Because of those hopes, I developed tunnel vision. That singular focus I found felt right because I knew that could lead me to the ultimate finish line. Education would open the doors to go anywhere in my life. I no longer wanted to be poor, and I wanted to help other people. If I could just continue to progress in school, I felt I could do both.

I attended Rancho High School, one of the three area high schools, and the one composed predominantly of Black and Hispanic kids. Today, the school is one of about 300 in the area, and it is nearly all Hispanic.

Being interested in your studies isn't usually the quickest way to find popularity. I didn't care. I maintained a constant state of focus and didn't waste a lot of time wondering about what people thought of me. I just didn't think much about what people thought, in a negative way. I probably thought more like, "Sorry for them." The way I conducted myself helped with the teachers, too. A lot of them took to me quickly because they could see how focused I was.

I didn't think I was particularly smart, but I began to make all As and Bs, so my classmates and teachers thought I was smart. My secret wasn't really any secret at all. I just studied hard. The teachers at Kubasaki didn't take any nonsense, and they had a high level of teaching compared to a public school. And I believe that my experience at Kubasaki High School had toughened me.

I was one of the few Blacks in most of my classes, and I found myself in the high-level classes with all the college-bound kids. That's probably why I didn't see too many Blacks. I could recognize that then, and I would spend much of my life trying to change that mentality.

Still, I had Black and White friends.

I can attribute that balance to me being an "Oreo," or at least being perceived as an "Oreo"—black on the outside, white on the inside. I suppose I was a little bit of an Oreo/egghead, but as soon as my classmates realized what a great athlete I was, I didn't catch any mess about being focused on my studies. Athletes get a pass.

Because I was focused on going to college, I figured I needed to have more than just good grades to have a college interested in me. Padding my resume with clubs and activities became important to me. I joined as many clubs and committees in which I could possibly partake. Included in that mix were the

Spanish Club, the International Club, Future Teachers of America, the Varsity R Club, and student council to name a few. I had fun being a part of those groups. Being a part of them made me feel special, like my classmates wanted my opinion. That made me feel connected and added to my confidence. I ran or walked the campus a lot and dreamed that maybe I could do the same thing in college. For a change, I almost felt in control of my destiny. In short, I think getting involved became a habit, a habit that would evolve into a lifelong habit. My total involvement continued in the community of Las Vegas as well as my complete involvement in NABSE.

My first year at Rancho High, I went out for track, but I had shin splints all year. I hadn't run track in Okinawa because it just wasn't an option. I'd never formally trained for track, which I think led to my physical problems. Because of those shin splints, I had a lot of second- and third-place finishes my junior year. People didn't know who I was after my junior season. My performance really shouldn't have garnered any attention.

That would change.

After my junior year, I went to visit my real father in Detroit. That was the summer of 1967, and to say that Detroit was in unrest would be a huge understatement.

Prior to going to Detroit, I'd been at a church retreat in California, and I'd seen a lot of what was going on in Detroit on the TV. Once my sister and I got to Detroit, we saw more.

That 1967 race riot in Detroit dealt mostly with confrontations between the police and Black people. The police raided an after-hours bar located on Detroit's Near West Side, which triggered violence that escalated into five days of deadly and destructive riots. Eventually, the Michigan Army National Guard arrived in Detroit as ordered by Michigan Governor George W. Romney. President Lyndon Johnson followed by sending in the Army's 82nd and 101st Airborne Divisions. Buildings were destroyed, 43 people died, and over a thousand people were injured.

Tanks arrived on my father's street, Epworth Boulevard. I could see them driving down the street. The TV coverage showed the burned houses and buildings, and all the looting that was going on. I said something to my father, like, "Hey, they got some TVs." That remark prompted a scowl and he added: "You better not even think of doing any of that!"

That whole experience brought about an odd mixture of emotions. I felt fear and wonder—empathy for those losing property, sadness for the poor, and respect for my father and those who were not participating. On top of all those feelings, I struggled with my understanding of civil rights issues.

Obviously, being older brought me more awareness. Some of that awareness concerned Daddy Walt's abusive treatment of my mother back at home. My brothers and sisters were used to hearing the loud talking and barking that Daddy Walt directed toward my mother. That alone brought a lot of stress. Of course, that's abusive behavior. But for the first time, I'd occasionally hear the hits. That alerted me to the fact that he used physical abuse as well. The physical abuse probably had been going on prior to me becoming aware of it. I probably just didn't understand what was going on, or simply couldn't put two and two together. One time I heard him hitting her, and I tried to stop him. That's when Daddy Walt hit me.

I'm not sure if abuse ran rampant in the neighborhoods we lived in, whether it was part of the Black culture or not. We never spent any time at other people's houses in the neighborhoods where we lived, so I couldn't really say. What I did know was that a healthy amount of abuse took place in my house.

Daddy Walt really didn't have a lot going for him when you stopped to think about it. An alcoholic who likes to fight and is abusive to his wife, that's pretty much being a lowlife. And one more thing, he liked to gamble.

The unlucky gamblers understand why all the casinos are shiny new buildings. That reason is simple: the casinos win the money. You might have a good day at the casino from time to time, but ultimately you dropped more money at the casinos than you brought home. The percentages aren't in the favor of gamblers. The house always wins.

Daddy Walt just didn't understand that fact. There were times when the man lost whole paychecks at the casino. That became obvious when I'd notice how distressed my mother would be after he'd gambled away the money. She needed to buy food, pay the rent, and take care of the kids. I'd usually hear her talking to him when she didn't think any of us could hear, or maybe she'd be telling a friend about how Daddy Walt had blown his paycheck. After that, I could see my mother trying to scramble together enough money to buy groceries.

Years later, I would try hard to forgive Daddy Walt and look for some redeeming qualities in the man. Today, I still have nightmares about him. My mother later told me that she thought that marrying Daddy Walt had been good for us in terms of all the experiences we had. Interesting enough, even though we never had much food, we always had food. I did thank him, not to his face, but I said we always had some semblance of a Christmas, even though it might not have been much. And he never drank in front of us, ever. Even though we saw the results of it. We never saw a bottle in the refrigerator or anything like that.

I did forgive Daddy Walt. I think being a Christian helped me with that.

After surviving everything, I figured we'd had a pretty good situation with all the travel. We always had a place to stay. The early years were in the projects, but still they weren't bad. And I didn't know they were projects, of course.

My senior year at Rancho High School began in the fall of 1967 and culminated with my graduation in June of 1968.

Running track my senior year brought out a totally different performance from me. I began to win. People wondered who I was, as if I'd just shown up at school. That was understandable based on my results my junior season. As a senior, I felt confident and I loved the feeling I got when I won.

I wanted to go to San Jose State because that's where future Olympians Tommie Smith and John Carlos went to school. I liked watching Smith run because of his technique. He was a thing of beauty.

I ran the 100-yard dash, and the 220. I won all of my races, but I couldn't break the 10.0 mark in the 100-yard dash. Any sprinter knew that you had to break 10.0 if you wanted a scholarship offer. That thought percolated in my mind throughout the whole season. I needed to break that barrier. Doing so would punch my ticket for college.

Despite the success I had in judo, and then track my senior year, I continued to fight low self-esteem. I guess that just boiled down to how I was wired, or what I'd experienced to that point in my life.

I didn't have any girlfriends. I thought I was ugly because I had a lot of zits, and I felt like I wasn't equal to other students I went to school with, for whatever reason. Most talk about their high school experiences as the best times of their lives. I basically had a sad and lonely high school experience. I didn't go out much at all, ever. My family didn't have a car until my senior year, which meant I couldn't just go anywhere I wanted to go. I either had to hitch a ride or walk to get to the track meets. For the most part, I stayed in the house, lay in bed, and read books like Steinbeck's *The Grapes of Wrath*.

There was one girl that I really liked, Andrea. I took judo from her father, Monte. I hoped to date her, but that didn't happen. We still became good friends, though. We'd hang out a lot. I plead guilty to being like a lot of guys in that I liked being around a pretty girl, even if she did not have any interest in me becoming her boyfriend. With Andrea, I got to observe the shoe being on the other foot, too.

Andrea was hopelessly in love with a Rancho High jock. If you look at the yearbook, he's on every other page. He did it all. Mr. Everything. The Most Valuable Player for the football, baseball, and basketball teams. He was even president of the student body. A lot of people made fun of Andrea for chasing after that guy. Being around her all the time, I let her cry on my shoulder about him, and I listened a lot. Andrea was Jewish, and I even went to the Temple once with her to pray. Over the years, she continued to keep track of me, and she has always made sure I got invited to the Rancho High reunions.

I went to the Air Force base chapel on a regular basis, and I had a Sunday school teacher who must have been intimidated by Daddy Walt, because he said, "Yeah, that father of yours, he's something." And he was a Black guy too. One day this man asked me if I wanted to leave the base to go to a Sunday school class. I did, and he took me to Sunday school and church off the base. That man's name was Sergeant Robert Trimble. He told me he wanted to introduce me to someone who could help me get a full-ride scholarship. That caused me to lose my breath. I'd never heard of such a thing. I'd been applying to a lot of colleges. I really wanted to go to one of the California schools. That's where all the fast guys in track were going. I could see myself competing against Tommie Smith. Man, I loved his style of running. Those long legs and arms were so free going around the track. I kind of thought I ran like him. But the responses to my applications to the California schools weren't good, so I gave up on that idea. I'd heard of people going to Arizona State and University of Arizona—great places for Vegas people to go, and I didn't get accepted there either.

My grades were low, which probably would have surprised my classmates at Rancho High School had they known. Remember, Kubasaki High in Okinawa. Even though I felt like my quality of education over there was amazing, they provided a foundation for my education, and they also taught me how to study, which made the Okinawa education experience worthwhile to my overall progress. However, that experience wasn't beneficial to my grades. I returned to the United States with some Cs and Ds on my transcript. When those were combined with my grades at Rancho High, I came out to less than a B average by the time I finished high school. That added to the anxiety floating around in my head. First, I didn't know if I could ever afford to get into college. Next, I thought if I could break 10.0 in the 100-yard dash, I could earn a scholarship; I just couldn't quite break that barrier. And finally, my grades. Could my grades earn me a spot in college even if I did break 10.0 and earned a scholarship?

Sergeant Trimble introduced me to a man who said he thought they could get me into the College of Idaho, and that I could probably get a free ride even though I didn't have a sub-10.0 time yet. I'd never heard of the College of Idaho, but I didn't care because they said I could probably get a free ride. I'm sure the guy probably knew I was poor as a mouse.

Eventually, Ed Bonaminio, the football coach at the College of Idaho, got involved. He said they didn't have athletic scholarships, but he thought they could get me the financial aid I needed provided I could play football. I told him I'd never played football before, so he asked me, "Do you think you can do it? I know you haven't played before, but we think you can learn. We'll teach you how." I said I'd do it.

Still, I didn't know for sure if I'd be going away to college by the time we went to the state track meet in Reno. I didn't know if I'd ever break 10.0, but I knew if I did it, that would improve my chances of going to college.

The Rancho Rams were underdogs at that state track meet. Only six of us qualified from our team. Several of the other high schools had a lot more athletes competing. Las Vegas High was the favorite.

We had to give up the prom to attend the state meet, but that really didn't matter much to me since I didn't have a girlfriend, nor did I have a date for the prom.

There were eight sprinters in the 100 final, including me. I felt confident. I'd been gaining speed throughout the season, and I was beating everybody. For some reason, I wasn't worried about not winning and what might happen to my scholarship if I didn't. I had focus. Winning the race was the only thing I had in mind. I wasn't concerned with who I was running against, which I never did. I think that single-mindedness kind of helped me. I didn't waste any time thinking about who the runners were in the other lanes.

When the gun sounded, I got off to a good start from the middle lane. Next thing I knew, I had broken the tape at the finish line first. Initially, I didn't know what time I'd run. When I found out my time, I was ecstatic: 9.9 seconds.

On top of that, we won the meet in a huge upset. The guys from Las Vegas High were pissed when we won and threatened that they were going to come over and beat us up because we'd won the meet.

Despite my thoughts about having to break 10.0 in the 100 to go to college, I did not celebrate early. I would wait until I got the final word to feel the relief of accomplishing that long-sought goal. I've always been a guy who pretty much had to see the eggs hatch first. But I felt like I had enhanced my chances.

The suspense about whether I'd get into college ended when Mike O'Callaghan called my mother. For whatever reason the future governor of Nevada called and talked to her, telling her, "Congratulations, your son is going to college." He must have known people from the College of Idaho.

During my senior year, I had been one of the finalists for the "Sun Youth Forum." The *Las Vegas Sun* sponsored this forum, which afforded kids an opportunity to discuss world topics. From that, a leader was chosen to write a column about the discussion. I got picked to write the column, and that had been a big deal because it got printed in the newspaper. I suspect that O'Callaghan had read my column.

My prayers had been answered. My goals had been met. I was headed to college. My chest swelled with pride.

# CHAPTER SIX

My life seemed to be coming together in the summer of 1968. I knew I'd be going to college, and, for the first time, I seemed to have a future. I also had a girlfriend—sort of, at least.

I'll call her "Ms. Rancho." We had gotten to know each other at high school. We talked a lot at student council meetings. I had not been able to ask her to the senior prom. The state track meet fell on the same day and prevented me from doing so. After graduation, she agreed to be my date at a dinner where the seniors got together and went to a German restaurant.

Going out with Ms. Rancho made me feel special. And that was back in the days when you only had one valedictorian. She was White. I'd never had any luck dating the Black girls at my high school.

We went to that restaurant and had fun, then we went out a few more times before I left for college. Of course, I fell deep for her. She attended the University of Santa Clara.

Given the way things were falling into place for me, I felt like a pretty happy camper prior to leaving for college. Ironically, this bliss on my part ran counter to the turbulent times taking place in the United States.

Martin Luther King got assassinated on April 4, 1968, at the Lorraine Motel in Memphis and on June 6, 1968, Robert F. Kennedy got assassinated at the Ambassador Hotel in Los Angeles.

When Dr. King got assassinated, I felt sad and disappointed. A voice for justice, peace, and hope had been lost. My sadness extended to all of America, not just for Black folks. We had followed the news on TV. I think I'd been philosophical, even before I studied psychology and sociology, thinking about people and how some thought one way and others thought another way. You get someone speaking the truth and then they're taken away. The injustice.

I had seen the hatred in the South as a kid, so what happened to Dr. King in Memphis did not surprise me. We were all depressed about when he got assassinated, and we really didn't know what to think. We also were frustrated at how the country could allow such hatred to manifest itself.

While Dr. King's assassination impacted all of us greatly, that event didn't impact us to the extent that the assassination of John F. Kennedy had earlier.

When JFK got assassinated, we were devastated. He had been a source of hope for the future for us.

My mother once wrote a letter to John F. Kennedy asking for help. My father was in jail when she wrote, so we were having a low time. She sent the letter, and he responded. That made us feel special. Gave us a personal connection, like the president was the kind of man who would respond to the people. When he died, we cried and were sad, not only for the tragedy of seeing the president of the United States killed, but his death made us feel as though our hope had been snatched away.

Kennedy had brought us more hope than Dr. King. We saw Martin Luther King as a preacher, who preached to the world. But we'd heard those same sermons in our church. While we saw King as a man who vented our problems to the world, we saw JFK as a man who could change the world. That's why JFK's death felt to us like a family member had died, giving us a real shot to the gut.

Shortly after JFK's death, I had a job selling commemorative JFK books. I'd always hustled. And I don't mean like cheating someone, I mean like out hustling getting jobs and that sort of thing. When that opportunity to sell those commemorative books presented itself, I grabbed it. We were living on the air base at the time. I'll never forget encountering a guy who nearly threw me off his porch when I tried to sell him a book. The idea of a JFK book pissed him off. He told me, "Get that trash out of here." I thought to myself, "Oh my God, some people really hate him."

That man's reaction taught me that everybody doesn't like somebody who appears to be doing good.

The Vietnam War raged amid that tumultuous summer of 1968. Protests were around every street corner. One segment of the country—mostly the youth, and my generation, had found a conscience, and wanted to make change.

Prior to leaving for the College of Idaho, I got an opportunity to work at the Atomic Energy Commission, the place where they do the bombs. On my job application, it asked if I'd ever been a member of the NAACP. That question brought me awareness about the country's conservative state. Once I got security clearance, I began to work there, which called for a lot of work just to get to work. I'd get up at 5:30 a.m. and ride the bus to an area east of Las Vegas. We wouldn't arrive until about two hours later. The ride was terrible, but the job was great.

I met some interesting people while working that job, which basically was a clerk job. But that didn't stop me from lifting boxes and getting my first hernia in the process. One of the FBI guys out there gave me a ride on one of those Vietnam helicopters—that was a pretty cool perk from the job.

Of course, you were served reminders about the place we worked when we got tested for radiation daily.

Speaking of Vietnam, I didn't want to go fight. I admit it. The prospect of going to Southeast Asia as part of a military fighting force frightened me. I remember thinking, "I don't want to go to that." I didn't believe in killing people and considered myself a pacifist. I wanted to go to school so bad. Everything mixed in to cause a lot of sleepless nights and plenty of anxiety. Everybody I knew my age tried in some manner to get out of going.

Hoping to get an exemption, I applied to become a conscientious objector. My first sixth-grade teacher, H.P. Fitzgerald, served on the draft board. I thought that gave me a better chance. But they denied my application. My status remained in limbo. I didn't know if I'd have to go to Vietnam or not.

Once the time came to head to college, I hopped on a bus from Las Vegas to the College of Idaho in Caldwell, Idaho. My excitement to get there got severely tempered after the first ten hours of the trip. That bus must have stopped at every cow town in Nevada and Idaho. The whole trip must have taken 24 hours. And I had thought the trips we took from Alabama to Detroit were long.

We finally reached Caldwell around midnight. The football coach, Ed Bonaminio, came out to this lonely bus stop to meet me. Nobody lived there, so the place was dark and quiet. Once we reached the campus, we got out of the car, and we walked to the Anderson Dorm, and he said, "Let's see, there's got to be some rooms over here." Whatever room he found for me, I remained there my first three years until I got an apartment.

Despite the surroundings and the hassles experienced traveling, I felt a sense of accomplishment. I'd gotten into college. I had entered a dream world on that campus.

The College of Idaho is a private, residential liberal arts college that was founded in 1891 and is the state of Idaho's oldest private liberal arts college. Because we'd moved around so much in my life, I wasn't scared in the least about living in a new town. Most of my fears stemmed from my insecurities about not making passing grades.

I'd developed good study habits by the time I got to college. Just getting to college demanded that kind of diligence with my studies. I didn't rest on my laurels. From the beginning, I just studied night and day. You had to study, simple as that. I'd gotten used to doing it from fifth grade on. That had been my mode, study all the time. Even in the summer, I read books. I guess I just had a high interest in learning. Still, my classes overwhelmed me. I continued to pray, "Please let me pass this." That feeling of thinking I would not make it didn't go away. And there were those who didn't make it past that first year.

We watched the 1968 Summer Olympics from Mexico City in October of my freshman year. Because I admired Tommie Smith so, I had more than a passing interest in seeing him run the 200-meter race.

Smith employed a smooth-running style that made sprinting look effortless. I pulled for him when he won the gold medal in the 200 meters, recording a world-record time of 19.83 seconds. Australia's Peter Norman finished in 20.06 seconds to take the silver and John Carlos ran 20.10 to take the bronze, giving the United States first and third finishes, and two athletes on the podium to receive their medals. When "The Star-Spangled Banner" began to play, the scene got interesting, providing an iconic moment for a generation.

Smith and Carlos bowed their heads and held up fists covered by black gloves in a "Black Power" salute. They did not wear shoes, rather black socks. Each of the athletes on the medal stand wore "Olympics Project for Human Rights" badges on their jackets. Later, Smith would say that the action had been a human rights gesture and not a "Black Power" salute. Whatever the case, the episode upset the applecart. People were appalled that such a radical action would take place while the National Anthem played.

I felt proud of Smith and Carlos even though the scene at the College of Idaho felt a little awkward since there were only about ten Black students at our college; eight were men. Most people didn't say anything, especially the coaches. But you would occasionally hear the comments like, "I hope they're not going to be like that." And I'm thinking, "I'm not that big of a protestor, but I sure sympathize with Smith and Carlos. And there's nothing wrong with what they're doing, because they're telling the truth by putting their fists up there."

Though I understood why they did what they did, I felt sadness. I knew they would be ostracized for what they'd done.

I've always wanted to understand the why regarding human behavior. I think my deep interest in psychology, sociology, and cultures evolved from me moving around from city to city. I thought Smith and Carlos were brave, and I thought they were standing up for justice. What they did took great courage, kind of like what Colin Kaepernick did in the NFL with his kneeling during the National Anthem. At the same time, I knew they'd burned a bridge they couldn't go back over. Burning bridges like that can lead to getting fired, or simply cutting off some possibilities for yourself. On the other hand, if you have that kind of conviction, and that's your mode of trying to promote change, then God bless you. Because few have the courage to stand for the many.

People suffer all the time when they step out. When Smith and Carlos did that, they had to do a little suffering. There are choices. But everybody does what they can. You need to be aware about what you can do and what your limits and strengths are.

I do remember digesting what they had done and thinking about the hopelessness that Black folks felt. I thought that it wasn't good that folks felt so helpless that they acted out the way they did. I thought we had to find a way for more people to find hope. I had hope, and just felt like you had to work hard. I felt more people should step up to prevent this from happening. Prevent the hopelessness.

Kids of the 1960s lived through a whole different time. Those were turbulent times, and sometimes scary. How did I fit into the 1960s? Well, I always saw myself as a peacemaker. I had been a strong student of the Bible. I saw a lot of the stuff through the eyes of the Bible—peace within and the storm will go around you. That's kind of what's always happened with me, even though I might have been sad through those times. God had always protected me no matter what I did. Just repeated miracle after repeated miracle.

I tried to provide an example of peace and love. I realized that I was good at forgiveness, and a lot of unselfish giving. That's one of the main definitions of love. And people just didn't see that. They didn't see that love is when you forgive folks, even when they're totally opposite of what you believe. My tolerance level for difficult or turbulent times has always run high dating back to my childhood.

Take Muhammad Ali. We just praised Ali. We made sure to drop whatever we were doing to listen to his fights on the radio. We thought highly about the stance he took. Most of the Black commentaries, Black newspapers, and Black discussions were about Blacks going to Vietnam representing the United States, yet we were still getting discriminated against here. We felt Ali's stance about not wanting to go to Vietnam had been valid.

I've never had a problem with those who chose to be revolutionaries. I've never had a problem with other people's ideas. Even if you took the Black Panthers.

The violence they brought didn't strike me as a good thing. However, I did understand the anger they had because there were many unjust things that were happening, kind of like how I see the Bible. God warned you and you disobeyed, so he killed all your siblings, all your kids. I wouldn't have wanted to be put in the position to be one of the killers, but I wasn't condemning the Black Panthers' activities, or any protesters for that matter.

Malcolm X once stated all White people are bad. I didn't agree that the White man was the devil, as the Muslims did at the time, but I was empathetic with that rhetoric, and thought it had some good in it. What we forget is that men are not God. They're not Jesus. They're not perfect. I do think that before you protest or have a cause, you need to get your strategies and your arguments together, so you can be more convincing as a group.

Of course, if you read all of Malcolm X's biography, you find out that he became a Christian. Muslims didn't want people to know that. And the media got more out of Malcolm X's "kill the Whites" than out of his conversion. He converted to Christianity. That's one of the main reasons the Muslims wanted him killed. The Muslims didn't want to tell their people that one of their main leaders had converted to Christianity.

When Malcolm X got assassinated, I didn't know that he had converted to Christianity. I gathered that later after reading the biography about his life.

I liked the whole notion of protest. I considered the protesting good and, at the time of so much protesting, I thought the protesting served as a good balance to Martin Luther King. Forgotten in time is the fact a lot of Blacks were against Dr. King. A lot of them were bothered by the fact Dr. King was out there "protesting and agitating." And, like I said, a lot of those who were upset with him were Black.

Although most considered Dr. King to be an agitator, I didn't consider him as such. Other Blacks did. And there were those Blacks who felt like his action made things hard for them, because

Whites would say, "You better not think like him." And Blacks would respond, "We don't think like him."

People like Malcolm X countered Dr. King's message with "You know, you could have a life for a life. Or a beating for a beating," as the Muslims would say. And "How would you like that as a way with dealing with discrimination? And beating children when they protest on the street. Releasing dogs on kids."

The Black Panthers' message made Martin Luther King and Malcolm X tougher to hear. They were like, "We're going to go out and strike before you get a chance to strike against us."

I understood it. I just didn't agree with their way.

I really didn't have a problem with Muslims, either. They did a great job of talking about cleaning yourself up and eating right, and this sort of thing. I just really didn't believe in their religion or anti-White stuff. But I thought they were a good balance for someone who had no religion or no hope at all.

Amid all the protesting, Vietnam remained on my mind.

I continued to feel tension about the situation. Were they going to snatch me out of college? My friend Everett "Slime" Carolina and I both thought we might have to go. Everett got the nickname "Slime" because he could find a way to get out of any situation. Slime was

Teflon—nothing stuck to him. We were both on the football team and became friends. We were two of the eight Black football players at our school.

The military needed young men like us. Remember, that was 1968. They were fighting the Viet Cong like mad at that point.

A sober kind of attitude prevailed, but I didn't really get to talk to a lot of the guys who went to Vietnam.

One guy from my Sunday school class went to Vietnam the year before I went off to college. I gave him my Bible, believing that would be the Christian thing to do. Particularly since I'd studied hard with that Bible. I'd highlighted passages and made notes. That young man died in Vietnam. Every time I've gone past that Vietnam monument, I've thought of him. Other than him, I knew an older guy, Naaman Foster, who played on the College of Idaho basketball team who'd gone. He never talked about what happened over there. But he was a jokester. He always called me "Bernie the Bullet." Everyone at the College of Idaho always called me Bernie, then later some would say, "Bernie the Bullet."

Since we were a liberal college the climate on campus remained anti-war. Joan Baez once visited our campus. Plenty of others arrived on campus to sing and hold anti-war discussions. We didn't do a lot of protesting, though. Mostly we had intellectual discussion-type stuff.

Later, when the lottery took place, my birthdate came up at No. 153. Coming in at such a high number prevented me from getting drafted. Slime's number came up a lot lower than mine, but his father worked for the government. I had heard that his father would get him out of having to serve. And sure enough, he didn't have to go.

Vietnam aside, I felt overwhelmed at college. I couldn't absorb enough of what I needed to absorb to do well. I just couldn't keep up. There was a lot of reading and a lot of expectations for tests and those sorts of things. Believe me, the College of Idaho was—and still is—a tough school. No doubt the college's reputation for always getting its students into medical school without exception had a lot to do with that. Still, I'd been through a lot in my life. Even though the odds looked like they were stacked against me, I just kept trying.

I never missed classes. You weren't supposed to miss classes there. They were small classes, run by loving professors. There were only 800 kids. You'd see the professors everywhere. They wanted to see you do well, and they wanted to see you get your degree. I liked the place, but I felt lonely up there my first year. I got the freshman shakes—I really was homesick. I think they felt bad for me because one of the coaches gave me a plane ticket to go home, even though the coach wasn't supposed to because of what you could and couldn't do for athletes. Again, they must have seen how bad off I was.

I remained a serious student and a straight arrow, always doing the right thing. Those who knew me, and some who didn't, called me "the narc," or the abbreviation for a narcotics agent, or informant. Given all the drugs and pot that students on campus were using at the time, I can understand there being suspicions of what took place in the dorm rooms.

One time, Slime, Richard Keys, Karlos Henry (Karlos and Richard were roommates), another friend, and I drove to Boise, Idaho. They started smoking a joint, and I told them, "Stop the car right now. I'm going to get out and walk. Just stop the car."

They could tell I wasn't kidding. That probably added to the suspicions about me. Kids were getting busted in college. They'd plant young policemen in the dorms so they could arrest kids. I can understand why some of my fellow students thought I was a narc. They were scared to be around me.

I remained obedient to my faith throughout my time at the College of Idaho. The big thing I struggled with: how do you stay a virgin?

That question remained a constant struggle. And I begin to think, "I don't want to stay a virgin. I want to get in the bed too."

Based on my desire to lose my virginity, I even considered becoming a hippie. I thought being a hippie, and going out to live in a commune, might be a pretty good deal—love and be loved. I thought that would have been cool. I kept meeting kids from California. Observing how laid-back they were, how they operated, and their penchant for sex. I don't think it would have taken much of a nudge for me to travel down that road. That opportunity never presented itself, though. Probably because I remained so focused on my studies, and because of my reputation as a narc.

I had very few dates, but most of that had to do with a girl I'll call "Ms. Caldwell." While Ms. Rancho and I would continue to have our little thing going on from a distance, Ms. Caldwell became my college dream girl.

We met my first year. Among other things, we were dance partners. She loved to dance, and we would dance all night long. I wouldn't have a date with her, but she would be like a date, because every time we had a dance at the Student Union Building, we would dance together. People would say, "Golly, that boy has energy." I'd have my classes, I'd work out, and I'd go to football practice, which should have tired me out. It didn't when it came to Ms. Caldwell, who was a cheerleader. I just loved her. I dreamed about that girl for four years.

Ms. Caldwell wouldn't date me. That frustrated me because my attraction to her made the prospect of dating anybody else difficult. During my senior year, I told her, "You don't have a boyfriend, why can't you date me now? If you don't want to date me now, I don't want to be your friend anymore."

She had tears in her eyes, so I thought I had a chance. But later she said we were different races and she didn't believe in interracial marriage. She seemed almost sad to tell me that. That hurt me and really disappointed me in Ms. Caldwell.

If she'd have told me that earlier, I don't think I would have thought about her all the time. But she'd been so nice to me, so I always figured I had a chance to be involved with her romantically. I do believe the fact that we became such good friends made me want to do better in school and have a double major in education and psychology.

I don't remember why I picked psychology. Maybe my self-esteem issues had something to do with that. When I took a psychology class first, I felt like taking that class would allow me to learn a lot about myself and others. Somewhere along the line, that class confirmed I should major in psychology. I said to myself, "Man, this is me. I've got to learn this."

As for majoring in education, I had a simple explanation: Ms. Caldwell majored in education. She influenced me, and I'll always remember her as one of the reasons why I stuck with the teaching curriculum. You had to take those basic classes. Since we had the same major, Ms. Caldwell and I had a lot of the same classes. I really hadn't intended to have anything to do with teaching. Certainly, teaching ranked only as a possibility.

Ms. Caldwell was Catholic, so I went to Mass sometimes with her at the Catholic church on campus. I didn't care for the Catholic rituals or else I would have gone with her more often. After being a good Baptist for so long, I found the Catholic church kind of dry. I still went to her church every now and then, and I remained strong about my beliefs. I still didn't drink any liquor.

Out on the football field, the fact I'd never played before became obvious. Was I fast? You bet. Nobody on the team could run faster than me. But when it came to the skills needed to be successful at football, I came up empty. I'd never tried to catch a football before, so when the quarterback zipped one in my direction, I didn't have a chance. I didn't like getting hit, either. Not exactly the best combination for a football player to have. I know the coaches loved the idea about the possibilities created by me when I sprinted past the defenders. Our quarterback would simply have to lob passes down the field to me for touchdowns. That prospect just never came to fruition.

Ms. Caldwell was from Hawaii, and there was a Hawaiian football player who liked her. I don't know how close they were, but every chance he got to hit me, he would. Whenever I saw that guy, I'd run the other direction. I constantly looked out for him.

Even though I couldn't pair my speed up with football skills, the coaches were nice to me. They tried to help me, but they didn't want to spend a lot of time teaching me now to catch. I ended up spending a lot of time on the sidelines. When we played games, they put me on special teams and had me play defensive end hoping that I might break through the line and tackle somebody because of my speed.

One of the highlights of my football career came in a game against Boise State. Of course, they didn't have the kind of program they have today, but, still, we were playing Boise State on November 23, 1968. And they came to our stadium to play. That would never happen today. Playing defensive end at one point in the game, I almost became famous. The ball got knocked out of the quarterback's hands and suddenly there it sat right in front of me. All I had to do was pick it up. As fast as I could run, I would have been in the end zone in a heartbeat. The guy who didn't even know how to play football would have scored a touchdown. But when I got to the ball, I stumbled trying to pick it up before I kicked it out of bounds. I didn't score a touchdown, but it felt great for the instant when it happened. People talked about that forever. Like, "Boy, Bernard, you could have had a touchdown against Boise State." I could just feel everyone on their feet in the stadium. Boise State won the game 16-7.

Aside from the fact that I wasn't any good at football, I found my experience as a football player quite interesting. Like I've said, I've always had a fascination with people. And let me tell you that football team proved to be a fascinating group to be around. There were so many macho rituals that were inbred in the game. On top of that, the effect that being on the football team had on me I now find comical. Suddenly, I felt like a man. Big tough guy. Remember, a big part of the attraction of judo came in the gentle foundation of the sport. I believed in the gentle sport. Judo is a gentle sport. You don't strike a person. When you throw them over your back, you gently drop them. In stark contrast, I'm suddenly wearing a helmet and shoulder pads, playing a game that ostensibly you had to be a tough guy to play. You had to be tough and hit people. I remember when I went home from college for Christmas break that first year, I would walk around like I thought a football player should. You know, "I'm tough. I know how to hit somebody." I felt like big shot. I felt like a real man. The way I carried myself, you would have thought that I played in the NFL. I strutted around like I was O.J. Simpson.

During the winter session of my freshman year, I signed up for a judo class. Believe it or not, I got credit for that class. That served me well, because for the longest time, I felt as though I would one day be a judo instructor. Over the years, my instructors had convinced me that I would be able to do judo for the length of my life. I thought that once I got out of college, I would be a teacher, a counselor, or whatever, but when I retired, I would become a judo instructor. I thought that teaching people how to defend themselves through this gentle sport would be a great pursuit.

Judo ended up being a year-round activity for me since I began to help teaching judo classes. Judo continued to come easy to me. Any time I spent on the mat felt like fun. I considered myself to be a lot better at judo than track.

Mr. Yamashito, who hailed from Japan, taught the class. He would bring in young Japanese instructors. They could barely speak English if they could speak any at all. I competed against them and that's when I got my black belt.

I finally grew out of my desire to be a judo instructor when my interest grew in other things.

When spring rolled around, I attended spring football practice and I also ran track.

Running track felt right. From the beginning, I beat everybody I raced. I knew track would work out well. Our track coach apologized to me about not being able to help me much. That kind of felt par for the course. I didn't think a whole lot about my speed, and the gift that God had given me. My mind-set probably had gotten shaped to think that way since I didn't think the school I ran for, nor the schools we competed against, were big-time. Big-time track athletes got scholarships to schools in California. Right or wrong that's the attitude I had and why I didn't take the whole thing that seriously. I pretty much expected to win every time I ran, and I did. I certainly didn't consider myself hot stuff for winning, because, again, I felt as though I was second tier. I did lose one race when I was a freshman, to a guy from Utah State. Big tall fella. I never lost again while at the College of Idaho.

I went on to win the Northwest Conference 100-yard dash in 1970, 1971, and 1972, along with the 1971 220-yard-dash title.

The only time it became semi-important came when a guy told me I was going to the NAIA finals my senior year.

We flew there in a private plane, and we almost crashed. Lightning cracked all over the place and the plane shook every which way. I hardly noticed because I had my nose in a book studying.

The pilot told my coach, "I know you want to get to where you're going, but we better land this thing."

We landed and waited out the storm.

We finally got to the track meet in Billings, Montana. I advanced to the semifinals and I won. After the race, I learned that I'd beaten Robert Taylor, who went on to make the United States' 1972 Olympic team. I got interviewed by famed long jumper Ralph Boston, who did TV. And he asked me, "Where have you been? I don't remember seeing you. That was some race, you beat Robert Taylor. You looking forward to the finals?"

I said, "Yes, thanks."

Ms. Rancho called that night. The conversation did not go well. Essentially, she delivered a Dear John letter with her words.

For some reason, I'd always felt like Ms. Rancho and I had something together and that we'd eventually get together. We were a long distance away from each other, since she was at Southern California. Maybe that's why our relationship lasted for as long as it did. I didn't really see her except for summers and holidays. We'd stayed together mostly on the telephone.

I kind of had a hint that Ms. Rancho's telephone call might deliver bad news. She'd come to visit me in Caldwell earlier that year. I'd detected a vibe, or a foreshadowing that things were not going well. She'd been a little standoffish. Our phone conversation validated my feeling. She'd fallen in love with somebody else. We broke up for good.

Taylor beat me in the finals and went on to represent the United States in the 1972 Munich Summer Games. I don't know if the outcome of the race would have been different if I would have been at the top of my game mentally. In the aftermath of the breakup, I certainly wasn't.

The most attention I got for my running while at the College of Idaho came during a meet at Oregon State. They competed at a higher level than us, so I shocked everyone that day when I got clocked at 8.9 seconds in the 100-yard dash. That time would have established a new world record. All the attention I received quickly became short lived. They measured the track and the distance came up short of a hundred yards by a yard. They estimated my time would have been about 9.3 on a regulation 100-yard track.

After my freshman track season, I figured that being good in track meant I didn't have to continue playing football. I quit the team before the start of my sophomore year, which proved to be a good thing for me—and the football team.

Even though I continued to run track through my senior year, and had success, the sport never meant much to me. The only time I really started to think about it was in the context that I should have taken advantage of my gift from God and practiced more. Academics were most important to me. Sports were no big deal. I never thought I had that much talent. I knew I wasn't as good as John Carlos or Tommie Smith; after all, they were at San Jose State, along with Lee Evans. They were coached by the legendary Bud Winer. Everybody knew that place as "Speed City." I was kind of anti-jock to be honest. I enjoyed running, and enjoyed sports a little bit, but academics ranked first with me.

Even if I'd wanted to continue in track, I knew I didn't have the money to do so after college. Back then, amateur athletes really were amateurs. So amateur athletes had a difficult time getting by without a paycheck of some kind.

Like any college student, I found time to be a precious commodity. Particularly since school remained a struggle.

I continued to hit my knees every night to ask God if he could see fit to get me through school. My sophomore year, I got some encouragement during the winter session while taking a class based on the history of the West. Everybody called the class "Cowboy Lit" and I found it fascinating.

We had to read ten or 12 books in six weeks. Initially, I didn't think I could take the class and do well. Still, I signed up. Everybody told me I'd like the teacher and that I'd find the class interesting. The teacher, Louie C. Attebery, became one of the English chairpersons, and though I struggled to keep up with the reading at first, I found the class fascinating, and I loved the teacher. I just stayed in my room and made sure I read those books. For all I know, that class is why I enjoy reading so much now. Even though I read a lot in high school, I'd never read like this before. I realized how much of a difference it made reading something that you enjoyed reading about. I logged that away for later in my professional career.

I had a benefactor in Robert Kaltenborn, who was a Las Vegas developer. Someone had told him about me and he had an interest in providing me with scholastic financial assistance. I visited him before I went off to school, and after. He's a historical figure in Las Vegas. Among his accomplishments, he developed a rich area of town, Rancho Circle, building expensive homes there. I met with him several times, and he seemed to take a liking to me. He gave me money to help pay for college. Then, when I got to college, he'd send me $300 or $400 from time to time. I don't know why. I guess somebody told him I was a nice guy and that I worked hard. I had a lot of saints helping me out in all kinds of ways. Other than helping me with money, he helped me with my reading by footing the bill for an Evelyn Wood speed reading class. That class wasn't cheap.

And he told me, "Hopefully when you go back to college you don't grow one of those goatees. That's a sure sign of subversive folks."

I knew Kaltenborn, who was White, had the Black Panthers in mind. "Because everybody who grows those goatees, they're radicals."

I thought, "Boy, he's a conservative sucker."

He really treated me well and I regret never telling him how much I appreciated what he did for me before he died.

Having the ability to read faster helped a lot. But I still couldn't see the light at the end of the tunnel. The prospect of graduating never seemed real. Even by my junior year, I still felt that way. Then I managed to survive some particularly hard classes. Those successes fueled me with confidence.

Religion ranked No. 1 among those hard classes.

A visiting professor from Germany taught the class, which added difficulty to the class. I couldn't understand a word he said. Nobody could. Slime, who I considered a smart guy, dropped out of that one. I would have dropped that class if I hadn't mapped out everything meticulously for what I had to do and take to get the hours I needed. I knew exactly what I had to take to graduate and that meant finishing those classes even if they were tough. I just read the King James version of the Bible as best I could. The Old Testament can be difficult to understand. I got a D in that class and I felt relieved not to have failed.

# CHAPTER SEVEN

Human behavior continued to be an interest of mine. Maslow was the big guy I followed in college.

Abraham Maslow came up with Maslow's hierarchy of needs, which originated in the paper he wrote in 1943, "A Theory of Human Motivation," that was published in *Psychological Review*. The gist of Maslow's hierarchy of needs is often captured in pyramid form, with the largest, most basic needs at the bottom. That ranges to the top, where after attaining everything below, the need for self-actualization gains importance.

Maslow's thinking resonated with me.

First, I felt like it followed the lines of Christian principles. In addition, from my upbringing, I knew what being at the bottom of that triangle of needs felt like.

My mind felt full of all kinds of theories at that stage of my life.

An impactful experience that would help direct what I wanted to do came my senior year when I had what amounted to an internship at the psychiatric ward in Pocatello, Idaho, where they had a state psych ward. Thinking about that place today still gives me the creeps. Among the more disturbing sites were the dungeons where they'd put patients on the beds and shock them. Pretty gruesome looking. I had a room in the place and stayed for six weeks.

At one point, they locked me up with the regular residents in a room that had eight to 12 beds. This was an experience for psychology majors to try to feel how the patients felt during incarceration. I was given my own bed and they didn't tell anybody I wasn't a patient. Talk about nerve racking. I went in there just after dinner, spent the night, and came out the next morning.

Another exercise saw them take all my clothes off, cover me with a sheet, then they laid me on a bed and locked up my hands and legs. I had to spend the night that way.

Being locked down overnight was like a psychedelic, mental thing. I wanted to get out of there so badly. All kinds of crazy thoughts went through my head. Like, "What if they forget me and think I'm a regular patient?" Everything went through your head, because I couldn't get out.

While going through both of those experiences, I worried about one of the inmates coming in and stabbing me or choking me. I felt so vulnerable in both instances.

During my time there, I met all these folks with problems, and they acted like they were normal. That's the thing about crazy folks; you can't tell something's wrong with them. I'd have these long intellectual discussions with these different people who were educated, but they had all kinds of craziness.

Turned out to be a good experience. Just like growing up an Army brat. You just never really learn what a person is like until you get to know them. After that, I thought to myself that I would have to think twice about doing that kind of work. I decided I'd go into counseling instead of becoming a psychiatrist.

I wanted to be a college professor at that point. The teaching, counseling combination at a college appealed to me. I always wanted to be an intellectual at a college. I did realize that I wasn't all that interested in the extremes.

I graduated from the College of Idaho with a Bachelor of Arts in Psychology and Social Studies in 1972. Only after I graduated did I fathom the quality of education I had received at the small private school.

Graduation ceremonies were special to me. I'd thought a lot about that moment since I first entertained the idea that someone like me could go to college. Not only go to college, but thrive in the college environment. Graduating from college brought the answer to many prayers. All my hard work to that point in my life got validated by reaching that goal.

My mother traveled to see me graduate. Daddy Walt did not make the trip. The biggest surprise came in the arrival of the Bear. My father attended my graduation, as did his wife. I guess he considered my graduation to be of great significance since it marked the first time my real father had traveled to watch or acknowledge anything in my life. I could not believe they came all the way from Detroit to the College of Idaho. But they were there.

Making the day more special were all the professors in attendance. Throughout my time at the school, I found that I could talk to them most any time in the small student lounge. When we graduated, they were proud we had done so. They'd taught us and nurtured us. They wanted us to succeed. When I did graduate, a part of them graduated with me. They had been a huge part of my success. I tried to take pictures with as many of my professors as I could, especially Frank Specht, everyone's favorite history teacher. He told the most detailed and fascinating stories about the kings, the queens, and the noblemen; he just made history great.

While my graduation brought a cause for celebration, I knew I had to start the next chapter, and I wasn't exactly sure what that would be just yet.

# CHAPTER EIGHT

After graduating from the College of Idaho, I decided I wanted to get my doctorate. I said to myself, "I didn't do the track right, so whatever it takes to get this doctorate, I'm going to do just that."

Grad school would be the first step.

I began applying to grad schools and wasn't having much luck getting accepted. Accordingly, I grew frustrated, or insecure, about not being able to get accepted. If I wasn't going to get into grad school, I knew I needed to get a job.

First, I got a recreation job working at a pool. I moved up quickly. They put me in charge of the money and taking up the time sheets for the lifeguards. While I worked at the pool, somebody told me about a job being available at the Spring Mountain Youth Camp located at the Mount Charleston area of Las Vegas. The kids incarcerated there weren't bad kids, they'd just gone off track a little bit. They stayed in this camp situation where they're with similar kids. They were 18, 19, 20 years old. Being at Spring Mountain gave them a chance to turn around their lives before they became hardened criminals. They were enrolled in school there, too.

Instead of being locked up, they were in a house with a counselor. I had 15 boys. Climbing down the mountain was the only way they could escape, and that presented a long climb for them. Still, they would try.

Once they hired me, I had my first salaried job, getting paid $8,200 a year in 1972.

I had to be totally hands-on, and somewhat like a fireman. I'd have three days on, four days off, and I'd be there 24 hours. Since I'd already gone through that nerve-racking episode at the psych ward while in college, I felt prepared.

I encountered manipulators, who were smart boys. One of them had made fake concert tickets and sold them. Slime would have fit in perfectly.

My judo served me well working that job when I had to use it on one of the boys. He was a tall, big boy, who tried to push me down. I put him on his butt and said, "Anybody else?"

I might have been a skinny little Black guy, but guess what, I could take down anyone. Nobody tested me after that.

My faith remained strong, but I didn't preach to the boys I wanted to help. I've always tried to show my faith by my example, and not by preaching any doctrines. I'm more into the "give them a fish and turn the other cheek" kind of thing, so they'd see the best way to go about living.

104

I continued to work at Spring Mountain because I still didn't know if a school would accept me or not. But I also continued to apply to grad schools.

Eventually, I got a call from the College of Idaho. They told me they'd heard I wanted to be a grad student, and that they had an opening for an internship. That made me feel great. Suddenly I knew I'd be able to pursue my master's. Then the University of Idaho called. That's when I received another miracle gift from God. They offered me an internship to go there while I earned my master's.

I discovered that my offer from the University of Idaho stemmed from my helping the Church of Nazarene High School track team while I went to the College of Idaho. When they held the banquet dinner for their track team, they invited me to attend, and I did. Prior to the program starting that night, they asked me to say the prayer, and I did. Throughout the evening, I chitchatted with the guy sitting next to me, who turned out to be the speaker. I don't remember what we talked about, but he was the athletic director at the University of Idaho. He remembered me and when he found out I wanted to get my master's, he recommended that I get a fellowship and scholarship at the University of Idaho.

While working toward my master's, I watched the 1972 Summer Olympics from Munich, Germany. That Olympics is remembered for the troubling terrorist activity that took place when Israeli athletes were held hostage. Some of them lost their lives. Those Olympics are also remembered for the confusion that cost a couple of American sprinters an opportunity to qualify for the finals.

Unbeknownst to U.S. track coach Stan Wright, he had an outdated schedule for the quarterfinal heats. Thus, his athletes were told the wrong time for when they needed to be at the track to compete. Neither Rey Robinson—who held the world record in the 100 meters at the time—or Eddie Hart managed to show up in time for their quarterfinal heat. Both were disqualified. The only one of the three sprinters to arrive in time for his quarterfinal race was a familiar name to me, Robert Taylor.

The U.S. sprinters had been watching the ABC Sports Olympic coverage while waiting for a bus to transport them to the stadium. While they were watching, they saw sprinters lining up for their race. Panic followed. Robert Taylor became the only one of the sprinters to make his heat, only because he had a later time for his heat than Robinson's and Hart's. He made it just in time, and managed to qualify for the finals, even though he barely warmed up. Taylor ended up winning a silver medal.

Seeing the guy that I'd once defeated drove home the message that I had not exactly put the gift God had given me to good use. I could have done more with my speed. Knowing that frustrated me to no end. I wondered if I could have been there in Munich with USA across my chest.

I remained in Moscow, Idaho, for two years while earning a Master of Education in Guidance and Counseling. I graduated in 1974 with my master's, then I began to apply for doctorate programs. I also started applying for other jobs.

Margaret Stewart had been my student teacher at the College of Idaho. She told me I should go after my doctorate, that I owed it to my people. I kind of forgot about it when I applied for teaching jobs in Las Vegas.

Mr. Nils Bayles, the principal of Eldorado High School in Las Vegas, told me if I would become a football coach, they would have an opening for me. I didn't want to be a jock, so I turned it down. I didn't know anything about football anyway. I just played one year. I still didn't know a thing about the sport.

Ironically, I eventually applied again to Eldorado High School.

Once again, they told me that the job would be mine if I took the football job. This time I said I'd do it, then I went and taught history for a year.

They filled my class up to the brim.

That first year at Eldorado High introduced me to having stress in my life. I broke out in hives. I worked way too much, grading essays late; training for the Olympic trials and coaching football didn't help matters, either. Finally, I quit coaching football after my second year. I told them I had the teaching job and I no longer wanted to coach football. So I didn't.

Adding to the stress, I had a girlfriend who moved in with me.

Susan and I had met in Moscow during my last year of the master's program.

I sighted Susan when she walked from the dorm. Immediately, I thought, "What a beauty." I introduced myself. Eventually she went out with me.

At that time, I no longer felt as restricted as I had. I'm thinking, "It's time for me to loosen up my morals."

Of course, the hormones were kicking in and running rampant. I couldn't stand my situation any longer. I wanted to be intimate with a girl. Susan became that girl.

She started coming to my apartment frequently. We became even closer when we got a late-night call and she found out that her sister had been killed in a car wreck. That was a tough night.

Susan's family lived in Idaho. Her father served in a prominent position and owned a little island. The place had clear water. We used to go skinny-dipping.

I really had a thing for Susan, I was crazy about her.

When I got the teaching job at Eldorado, she followed me to Las Vegas.

Ultimately, the fact she wasn't a Christian played a role in our future together.

Since she wasn't working, she would go home now and then. One time she returned from one of those trips and I could tell we needed to talk. Other things were on the table, but I never could get past her stance on religion. She was an agnostic. I think we both felt something was not quite like it should be, so we broke up. We were matched up culturally, but we didn't match up spiritually.

During my first year of teaching at Eldorado, I noticed the kids couldn't read, so I tried to be creative. I had the kids act out the history lessons. Then I had them read Malcolm X and James Baldwin. The vice principal, Georgeann Rice, got wind of what I had them reading, and I got written up.

"You're teaching this subversive, violent stuff," she told me.

I told her I had juniors in high school who couldn't read and that I'd tried to get them excited about reading by introducing them to some interesting stuff. I concluded, "At least they're trying to read the books I got."

She rewrote my evaluation and gave me credit for creativity.

During my second year of teaching at Eldorado High, I got a call out of the blue from the principal at William Orr Junior High School. He asked me to interview for a position they had as a counselor. I told him of my involvement with the Eldorado girl's track team, which I wanted to continue. He told me not to worry. I could work the counselor's job he was offering me and still be their coach. After that assurance, I jumped to accept the position.

A former teacher I'd had in high school had recommended me for the job. He'd watched firsthand how I'd worked to learn algebra. That subject had been a challenge for me, so I'd occasionally attend the same class, taught at another period, so I could learn it. I guess he admired my persistence.

Thus, I became a counselor earlier than the norm for a teaching career. Most places wanted you to teach five years before taking on a job like that. Timing is everything, and it worked in my favor in this case, so I left Eldorado midway through my second year to move to William Orr Junior High for what I considered a wonderful opportunity.

Unfortunately, once I got to Orr, I didn't like the plan the principal had for me. He had me teaching three classes and trying to be a counselor for the other three periods. I came to the realization I wasn't happy at my job. I attributed that in large part to the fact I didn't really like the principal. Nobody got along with him because of the way he tried to intimidate everybody. That guy really was a tough old bird. Coming to the realization that I did not want to work in said conditions, I started applying for other jobs.

I remembered an offer from the past and made a call to the superintendent of Las Vegas schools.

I'd run into the Las Vegas school superintendent, Kenny Guinn, inside the Eldorado school gym. That's the same Kenny Guinn who became 27th governor of Nevada in 1999. He came up to me and said, "Hey Bernard, wouldn't you like to work at the central office where I work someday?"

The offer caught me off guard. "Would that mean more money?"

"Yes," he said.

I told him I'd think about it. I didn't know anything about the central office, so I kind of tucked that offer away.

When I called him, I asked if he still had an available job for me. He told me he'd send somebody over to talk to me. That same day, the assistant superintendent came to me and offered me a job. The following fall, I started as special programs counselor coordinator.

I spent the next four years at the central office, which proved to be a great experience for me, and allowed me to meet Jim Pughsley, a man who I would look to as a mentor. In addition, I didn't feel the stress like I had at Eldorado thanks in large part to a fortuitous meeting with Thurman Warrick. After meeting him, I found my way back to the track and I began to run seriously again. Thurman had coached the Barbados Olympic team, and he became my coach, and he introduced me to Ken and Kermit Bayless. They were twin brothers, they ran the quarter, and they became my best friends. Kenny later became well known for being a boxing referee. We began working out together and started the Las Vegas Striders Track Club. The head track and field coach at the University of Las Vegas, Al McDaniels, would let us use their track. Working out at UNLV felt like paradise compared to the other places where I'd run track. It wasn't the track so much, because I'd run on a lot of nice tracks at meets. What impressed me most were the workouts. They were so much different. I said to myself, "So, this is a real workout."

I'll give you an example. Wednesdays you'd run around the four streets that enclosed UNLV at the time. That's a five-mile run—for a warm-up. We were timed and expected to really push. Then we'd go to the track and do a hundred 100s on the grass at three-quarters speed to get our legs ready. That would be just one workout. We'd also do weights that day. Some days we'd run in the mountains at 5:30 in the morning to get a break from the Las Vegas sun. Those workouts were the kind you used for Olympic and world-class training, a far cry from my college workouts.

We'd pool our money, and our coach would look for important meets that would give us an opportunity to eventually get to some of the Olympic trials if we did well enough. They had various races that qualified as pre-Olympic trials. We went to some of those, but we didn't break through to the big time.

Still, I got the idea that I might be able to earn a spot on the Olympic team, so I started training for that.

Thurman taught me how to get a better start, and that new start was out of this world. Once I had that start in my skill set, I said, "Holy moly, this old guy is really fast."

I began racing in big events and managed to race against some of the best. Among the notables I raced against were Houston McTear, Harvey Glance, Dr. Delano Meriwether, and Steve Williams.

Hailing from the Florida Panhandle, McTear burst onto the track scene in the mid-1970s, becoming an international track star. While

McTear's name could be found in the top ten for the 100 meters, shorter distances were his strong suit. In 1978, he set a world record in the 60 meters, covering the distance in 6.54 seconds. McTear's record held until Ben Johnson set a new one in 1986.

Glance twice tied the 100 meters world record of 9.9 seconds in 1976, and he finished first in the 100 meters USA Olympic Trials in 1976.

McTear and Glance both were slated to go to the 1980 Moscow Summer Olympic Games before the United States decided to boycott the games due to the Soviet Union's invasion of Afghanistan.

Dr. Meriwether became the first African American to graduate from Duke Medical. He became the 1971 track and field champion in the 100-yard dash. Later, he became well known for being the head of the United States Government immunization program during the 1976 swine flu outbreak.

Williams never reached the Olympics, but he matched the men's world records in the 100 and 200 meters.

Under Thurman, I became a much-improved sprinter.

Harvey Glance beat me in a race in 1978 when I ran a 10.1 in the 100 meters to finish second or third. Afterward we were talking, and Harvey said, "Bernard, I wish I had your start." And I said, "I wish I had your finish."

Clearly, my window of opportunity had closed for me to advance to the Olympics, but I did receive some acclaim during that period, including a mention in the April 1978 edition of *Track and Field News*.

McTear adorned the cover of that issue with the caption, "Fast."

Peeling through the pages of that issue, you can see photos of the track stars of the day highlighted by the likes of Renaldo Nehemiah and Curtis Dickey, who both went on to play in the NFL, too; marathoner Bill Rodgers; Dave Wottle; and McTear.

Under the section "1978 US Outdoor List," the magazine explains: "As this list shows, the 1978 U.S. outdoor season is wasting no time in getting underway. Already, those fortunate enough to have been able to compete in the warmer climes have produced a spate of notable early-season marks."

Under the "Men" list is a category for 100 meters. With a time of 10.33 seconds, Andrew Banks and LaNoris Marshall are listed first, followed by Clancy Edwards, Jerome Deal, and Mike Roberson.

The next category under "Men" is for "Hand Timing" recorded times. In the top spot at 10.1 seconds in the 100 meters are the names Bill Collins, Dickey, and yours truly, Bernie Hamilton, of the Las Vegas Striders Track Club.

My experience running with the big boys demonstrated to me how close I'd been to becoming a legitimate Olympic star in the sport. While I would have benefited from having the start that Thurman taught me all along, I once again surmised that I had simply not put in the work it took to become a champion and that I had squandered a gift God had given me with my legs. Going forward, I understood that attaining rewards and reaching goals were all about putting in the work. Not making the Olympics taught me you can do whatever you want. Once again, I set my sights on getting my doctorate. I needed persistence. I had not been persistent early on in my track career and I lost my gift. All it is training, and persistence, and you can achieve anything you want. I said to myself, "Whatever it takes to get this doctorate, I'm going to get that. I had an opportunity and didn't take advantage of it."

For four years, I worked at my job as special programs counselor coordinator. I gained my administrative credentials in the process. My job basically called for me to take care of all expulsions. I would interview literally every kid who got kicked out of school and sent to an alternative school. I reviewed all the paperwork for those kids.

116

In some cases, I got calls from court judges and I had to get reports to them. Or they told me what I wasn't going to do at the central office—you need to do this for this kid, or that. You're not providing enough services for them.

The job also called for me to meet with a lot of parents.

Some days I might meet with as many as 25 parents. They wanted me to determine whether the school had been unfair in dealing out the punishment they did. If they were being unfair, I'd call the school and tell them, "Your paperwork is out of order, this kid has to come back."

No surprise that I gained some enemies that way.

Thinking of my future, I made sure to go to every school board meeting. That experience proved to be the best education I had. I met some important mentors, too. During those four years, I learned a lot about the school district and administration. I ran a drug program and an attendance program. Toward the end of my tenure, I thought I'd gained the experience I needed to become a principal. By then, Kenny Guinn had left his position as superintendent, and Dr. Claude Perkins had taken over the job, becoming the first Black school superintendent in Las Vegas.

I asked Dr. Perkins if he thought I had a chance to move up. He suggested I get my doctorate. I'd applied at the University of Idaho, but I wasn't accepted the first time I applied. Mind you, my student teacher, Margaret Stewart, and I still talked from time to time. She expressed her surprise that I had not been accepted there before. Remember, she's the one who had told me, "You need to get your doctorate to help your people."

Margaret told me she planned to send a letter to the University of Idaho recommending that they reconsider me. Shortly thereafter, I got accepted to their program, putting me on track to get my doctorate.

Once I got to Moscow, Dr. Eldon Archambault said, "I don't know who this Margaret Stewart is, but she wrote a hell of a letter for you. That's the reason you got in."

Thus, in the summer of 1980, I left my job at the central office. I took intensive classes, and a one-year residence with two summers of intensive classwork. The university allowed my two years of master's work in counseling in 1974 to become part of my five years of continuous study at the University of Idaho. Therefore, at the end of the summer of 1981, I graduated with my doctorate in educational administration.

Prior to finishing, I got a call from the principal of Bonanza High School, one of the largest high schools in Las Vegas. He offered me a job as a dean at the high school. He thought I could handle the job.

118

Getting asked to do this job turned out to be a miracle blessing. There were two deans, and I served as the dean of discipline. The other dean handled attendance issues. Another piece of luck came in the fact that JoAnn Pughsley, my mentor's wife, was an assistant at Bonanza.

Bonanza High had almost 3,000 kids. That didn't deter me. I became hell on wheels at that job, and the kids loved it. I had a good time, too. I did my thing. I walked the grounds every minute of the day. If a kid got in trouble, I'd march him off to the parking lot and have him pick up every piece of paper he could in the hot sun, make him as miserable as possible.

I worked from Bonanza High from 1981 through 1982 before I left for Lois Craig Elementary School and Madison, where I worked as an administrative assistant, assistant principal in training. They told me I'd make more money, and they'd train me to be an elementary principal. Later I found out that the new principal of Lois Craig would be no other than JoAnn Pughsley.

Looking at my skill set, I knew I had to learn to teach reading, so I joined a curriculum group. That also taught me how you picked a book. I learned what the components of reading and writing were. The next year they assigned me to two different schools and I learned how to teach the components of reading. Through those assignments as an administrative assistant, assistant principal in

119

training, I learned what was expected of a principal by being an administrative assistant and an assistant principal in training.

After three years, I began to apply for a lot of different jobs.

Sometime during this period, I encountered an opportunity that would change my life. I found the National Alliance of Black School Educators—or they found me. Either way, NABSE felt like the perfect fit.

A nonprofit national organization founded in 1970, NABSE devoted itself to furthering the academic success for the nation's children, particularly children of African descent.

Dr. Hershel Williams, one of the main founders of the Las Vegas chapter of NABSE, called me and asked me to join him at a local meeting. Don Smith, NABSE's national president, and George McKenna, a famous principal at the time, were going to be speaking at the meeting.

McKenna gained fame after Denzel Washington starred in a movie that told his story. He'd been a teacher in Los Angeles before becoming principal of George Washington High School, a place where gangs and drugs impacted the students' lives.

McKenna wanted to offer quality education to his students, but he faced long odds, in part because of teachers and parents who couldn't or wouldn't offer the needed support.

The movie came out in 1986 as *The George McKenna Story* and later was re-released on home video under the name *Hard Lessons*.

When McKenna talked, I listened to how he ran his school. One day I wanted to run my own school. With that idea in mind, I always listened to gather ideas to better my school once I had one.

Every NABSE session after that, including when I went to the National Conference, became a huge deal for me.

NABSE sought to establish a coalition of African American educators, administrators, and other professionals, who were directly and indirectly involved in the educational process; create a forum for the exchange of ideas and strategies to improve opportunities for African American educators and students; and identify and develop African American professionals who could assume leadership positions in education and influence public policy concerning the education of African Americans.

NABSE strived to achieve its mission through three primary areas of focus: professional development programs that strengthened the skills of teachers, principals, specialists, superintendents, and school board members; information sharing around innovative instructional and learning strategies that had been successful in motivating African American youth and increasing academic performance in critical learning areas; and policy advocacy to ensure high standards and quality in the public and private education systems.

NABSE had me, and I felt committed for the long haul.

I found the organization's dedication to fighting the image that kids couldn't learn fascinating. They stressed that all Black kids could do well; they didn't have to settle for second class. I bought into that and I still do.

As I listened to the organization, I discovered there were all types of things about how boys learn differently than girls. How if you gave the right education curriculum, all kids could do well, and you could eliminate special ed, because everybody had certain gifts; the individual just needed to work on those gifts.

NABSE had captured me with its principles and I attended all the meetings. Next thing I knew, I became the vice president of the local chapter. A lot of stuff was happening in Las Vegas at that time.

# CHAPTER NINE

My time finally arrived in 1984 when I got assigned to be the principal at Walter Bracken Elementary School, which had been deemed a low-performance school. I happened to see something on TV about the school, and I noticed graffiti all over everything. The news reporter also showed cars parked around the school that had their windows knocked out presumably by gang activity. I'm thinking, "I'm going into a mess." But I felt the NABSE professional development experiences and my school experiences would serve me well at Bracken School.

At a school board meeting when my new job was announced, one member told me, "I still don't think you can be a principal." In other words, some of the board members didn't want me. Part of the problem with some of them was the fact I was active with local civil rights. They totally underestimated my resolve. I had a lot of fire in my belly at that stage of my life.

One board member, Mrs. Virginia Brewster, was very supportive. She was known throughout the city to advocate strong academics for all children, especially those in her district.

Once at Walter Bracken, all the years of studying and working at different schools began to pay off for me. I felt myself growing while I developed my own style.

I had high energy and felt wide awake on everything that came across my desk. And I continued to strive to understand all I could about educating students. I read everything. The *New York Times*, all the magazines on education, and I attended countless professional development conferences and classes with some of the best teachers in the country.

A lot of educators at that time embraced the effective schools movement. Most didn't know that a Black fellow named Ron Edmonds originated the movement.

The 1966 Coleman Report prompted the effective schools movement through its conclusion that the critical determining factors for student achievement were socio-economics and family background.

Christopher Jenks's published research in 1972 added to Coleman's assessment, noting that the quality of a school had little effect on a student's achievement.

Edmonds didn't believe the Coleman Report's findings were irrefutable. He allowed that socio-economic background couldn't be ignored as a factor affecting the individual student. What he didn't like was the idea of professional educators throwing their hands in the air and deciding such students could not be taught because of their circumstances. In contrast to the Coleman Report, Edmonds felt schools could make a difference.

Hoping to back his belief, Edmonds sought to find schools that had found success teaching children from low-income families. He managed to find schools where students had succeeded and compared what those schools were doing to what unsuccessful schools were doing. Through those comparisons, Edmonds uncovered things being done at the successful school that weren't being done at the schools that weren't as successful. Edmonds published "Effective Schools for the Urban Poor" in 1979, and the following characteristics were identified for effecting success: high expectations, strong administrative leadership, basic skills acquisitions as the school's primary purpose, an orderly atmosphere, and frequent monitoring of pupil progress. Those characteristics came to be known as Edmonds's "five-factor model" and they were embraced as a means for change at low-performing schools.

Edmonds had been determined in finding evidence that backed his belief that all children could learn, and he managed to do so. He once noted: "We can, whenever and wherever we choose, successfully teach all children whose schooling is of interest to us. We already know more than we need to do this. Whether we do it or not must finally depend on how we feel about the fact that we have not done it so far."

I embraced what Edmonds believed. Thus, I welcomed meeting Lawrence "Larry" Lezotte—a contemporary of Edmonds—when he arrived in Las Vegas. After getting introduced to Larry, he trained my teaching staff and me. That information complemented the message I heard from NABSE.

Since I served on at least ten organizations, managing my time brought a challenge. But I had passion. I wanted to change images.

For example, my school had a bad image, and everybody always talked about how the Black boys don't have a role model. I decided to invite a hundred Black males to the school. I wanted the young Black boys to see some impressive role models. Of course, the naysayers said nobody would come. This was before the Las Vegas community started the first "100 Black Men" organization, which was a national affiliate.

Some people just want to be negative.

Las Vegas never has rain. Yet on the big day, when the hundred Black males were scheduled to make their visit, it poured. Well over a hundred showed.

That gave me a lift, made me feel as though I was helping a lot of people.

Just as I'd been for most of my life, I continued to bury myself in a lot of activities.

What motivated me to be involved in all the organizations, the committees, and the volunteer activities? I'm not sure. In high school, I had done the same thing. I just had energy. I thought being involved would be a good thing, like being in the Spanish Club. I also knew that being on committees and being involved in different activities would help me with scholarships. But I liked being involved, too. I just gravitated toward being a part of things and I found such activities stimulating.

As an adult, I think being involved—active and doing a lot of stuff—had just become a habit. Doing so gave me a sense of fulfillment, too.

In addition to my involvement with NABSE, I had volunteered to become the chair for the education committee of the NAACP. I found out that nationally, they had a program for kids with talents called ACTSO (Academic, Cultural, Technological, Scientific Olympics), which I found fascinating. They had multiple categories in which young people could compete locally, statewide, and then at the NAACP national convention. They then could win thousands of scholarship dollars, or they might get chosen by a company like General Electric, or somebody else, to do internships. Some would even get their entire college education paid for. These students were the cream of the crop from the whole country. I organized ACTSO in Las Vegas and took kids to their national conferences in July. Attending those competitions, you might hear some of the best music you've ever heard, or see a creative science project, a great oration, or a painting.

As a member of the NAACP and the League of Women Voters, I walked neighborhoods registering citizens to vote. Other organizations had similar community service. I worked as a member of the American Association of School Administrators (AASA); the Nevada Association of School Administrators (NASA); Phi Delta Kappa (PDK), a prestigious educational organization; the International Reading Association (IRA); a trustee with my church, Second Baptist; and served proudly as the secretary of my beloved Kappa Alpha Psi fraternity (which I joined as an alumni member in 1981 while in Las Vegas). I also served as the chairperson for the education committee of the NAACP. Then I joined the Martin Luther King committee, which was new. Somebody suggested that I run for vice president of NAACP. After conferring with my mentors, I did, and I won. In less than a year, the guy who was elected president of the local NAACP got the national NAACP upset because he wasn't following their policies. Among the things he did, he called for a boycott of the Strip in Las Vegas. Of course, that upset the Strip people and prompted a visit to Las Vegas by the NAACP's national vice president. Once he arrived, his first order of business was to take away the presidency from the president. Since I was the vice president, he chose me to be the successor. That's how I became the president of the local NAACP.

Hoping to change the image of the organization, I decided to go on TV. I conferred with Ray Willis, the school district's public information officer, who told me I could get on TV to do free public announcements. I'd go on TV, I'd look at the camera, and I'd say, "Hi, I'm Dr. Bernard Hamilton. I'm the president of the NAACP and we have lots of programming to benefit our youth and community."

By doing that—and presenting the image of someone who was articulate and clear minded, I helped change the image of the organization. A lot of people knew me because I'd grown up in Las Vegas.

Through my activities, particularly my TV spots, I became one of the most influential Blacks in Las Vegas.

Two or three young folks running for office visited me to ask for my endorsement and for advice. One even went to the governor, and the governor told him, "Why don't you talk to Bernard and then come back to me."

Being involved also opened the door for me to meet my wife, Judy Lynn Graves.

Just prior to the announcement of my appointment to Walter Bracken Elementary, I was attending an NAACP meeting at the first Black elementary school in the area, "West Side School." The building had been turned into a radio station, KCEP, but it remained a historical building. TV people were there, and they were about to interview me when I spotted Judy as she entered the room.

Judy's sister taught at Chaparral High School in Las Vegas. A friend of Judy's sister suggested they come to watch the NAACP meeting. Judy walked in, her hair hung to her waist, and she had this beautiful smile. I put off the interview and I asked, "Who is that lady?"

A friend of mine, Paul Meacham, president of the Clark County Community College, brought Judy over and introduced her. That led to me to ask her if she wanted to go out for some tea. Her whole family has teased me ever since. "Who invites somebody out for tea? In Vegas?"

I didn't drink, or if I did, it was very little. We went to the Sands Hotel later that week to have a snack. I've always teased her about why she wanted to go out with me. She told me I seemed like a man on the move and that she just got interested. Her father had been an NAACP president, so that might have had something to do with the attraction.

She had been thinking about changing jobs and figured she'd visit her sister and explore Las Vegas as a possible place to work.

Judy had a quiet and reserved manner. She was different than everybody else. I could tell she was religious, too. She was so proper in her speech. She didn't get excited about stuff. We were opposites in a lot of ways. Even now she's very quiet. Very reserved.

Judy's father and grandfather had been heavily involved in civil rights when she was growing up in West Point, Mississippi.

Her grandfather had been the son of a slave. His mother was White, his dad was Black. He inherited a couple hundred acres of land that had been slave land in West Point.

Judy's family decided they would be the family to integrate West Point in the 1960s. That decision led to them being scorned and ridiculed. And they lost their jobs.

Because they were a talented family, they knew how to farm. They grew their own crops. They built their own homes. They even worked on the water system. Knowing how to do all of that made them self-sufficient and allowed them to sustain themselves when they lost their jobs. But going through what they endured had been demeaning.

Judy had been the only Black in her class and one of two Blacks in the school when she began second grade.

Her grandfather had the Freedom Fighters watching over them as they walked her to school the first few days. When they finally started having a bus, they got the bus to come by their house. Half the time, she would be in place waiting for the bus, and the bus would drive right by her.

Being an outcast, she had an isolated existence with no friends during elementary school. She ate and played by herself for five straight years because of the integration issue.

Once she got to middle school, her situation improved. Then in high school, it got a lot better. Her experience had a lot to do with shaping who she was.

After about a month or two of dating Judy, I said, "You want to get married?" She pointed out that we had just met.

We continued to date.

Judy loved movies, and so did I, so we went to the movies a lot. She went with me on some trips where we chaperoned the kids from the NAACP ACTSO competition. We took them to an ACTSO program in California and one in New York. She liked to travel. Because of my involvement in so many different organizations, most of our dating happened at activities for those organizations.

We were married in March of 1985.

## CHAPTER TEN

Getting married settled me down quite a bit. I loved having a wife, and we looked forward to starting a family. Being married also afforded me the opportunity to really concentrate on work.

As I said earlier, the graffiti at Walter Bracken had been everywhere when I arrived in the fall of 1984. Because my best friend, Bruce Theriault, worked as the director of the housing project in the area, I went to him seeking help with the graffiti. I told him I wanted all of it gone even if somebody had to do something at midnight, I wanted it cleaned up. I didn't want any of my kids to see any graffiti on any walls, ever. Bruce said he'd take care of it and he did.

I cleaned up the school physically, then I worked on my students' self-image. I wanted them to feel like they were as good as anybody else. Ron Edmonds's "five-factor model" served as a pretty good compass for how I proceeded.

The school composition as far as ethnicity broke down to a third Hispanic, a third White, and a third Black. Eventually, I wanted to achieve the same ratio among the faculty, because I believed in that role model stuff taught by NABSE. I also tried to bring aboard men, who were tougher to find than women.

Most of the teachers were White. When teachers were replaced, I tried to make a change, hoping to work toward the ratio I wanted.

I went to classes in the morning and in the afternoon to keep an eye on what was taking place in the classrooms. One of the things that I learned was that you do a lot of looking. I adopted some techniques from some of the best principals in Vegas, like taking notes and leaving a message.

When I'd walk through, I'd pass along a note to the teachers when I left their classrooms. I'd always write the good stuff first, something like, "I like the way you did the bulletin board. And the way you lined your kids up, you were so positive." On and on. I'd give them three or four things I liked. When I saw something I didn't like, I'd say, "I noticed that you didn't have your lesson plans done. Don't forget you need to have your lesson plans and they need to be on the desk when I come by." I strived to be consistent. The teachers who didn't like my approach eventually left. And the ones who didn't do what I asked them to do, I continued to write them more notes.

I took advantage of a policy that allowed me to visit other schools, and I did so frequently. When I made my visits, I'd make sure to let the teachers at those schools know that I had openings for this job or that. Before I knew it, I had stolen some of the best and brightest teachers in Las Vegas. One principal told me, "Don't be coming to my school trying to steal my teachers."

I did receive blowback from some White faculty. Still, I ended up with what I wanted, a group of teachers with a composition that was a third White, a third Black, and a third Hispanic.

When I first started at Bracken, I asked my teachers to volunteer to go to Boulder City, a little casino in Boulder City, Nevada, for a three-day weekend retreat.

We went to the retreat to be together and learn how to become an organization that works together. At the end of that retreat, I used effective schooling strategies to merge the whole school into three committees. They came up with a theme: "We work together, and we learn together."

Everybody served on a committee. One committee might be staff development, another, school environment, another, academics, etc.

Every function of the school would be reviewed by those teaching committees, including the budget. If you saw a piece of paper on the ground, you were supposed to pick it up. Everyone was on board. It just became a loving school.

We put out a parent handbook that outlined school policies, expectations, and the like. In the front of the publication, which was sandwiched between orange covers, was our mission statement: "Our mission at Walter Bracken School is to provide all children with learning strategies which guarantee maximum achievement in their academic and character development."

Underneath "Walter Bracken's Guarantee for Maximum Learning Achievement" we had the following:

Walter Bracken Elementary School agrees to:

Provide all children with learning strategies which guarantee maximum achievement in their academic and character development.

Employ professionally trained teachers and staff who will give individual attention to your child's needs.

Organize a school which emphasizes student self-respect, self-responsibility and respect for the rights of others.

Provide the needed textbooks and other related learning materials.

Emphasize academic excellence by rewarding academic achievement.

Provide monthly progress reports to keep parents and students informed of their progress.

Provide update methods and strategies to guarantee improvement of your child's achievement in the basic skill areas of reading, writing, and arithmetic.

A signature line came at the end that read, "Dr. Bernard Hamilton, signing for all staff."

In addition, there were also places on the page for parents and kids to agree to certain things, including a signature line for them to sign.

The page concluded with the following:

"In our plan for improvement in student achievement at W. Bracken, we find that it will take a three-way effort from the staff, the parents and the students, themselves. The intent of this agreement is to hold each significant party responsible. Together, we will monitor your child's progress, and if there is a slacking off, we will ask, 'Who's been falling down on the job?' This Learning Guarantee is only effective if all participants accept the responsibility as listed."

Academically, we were low. But I said we were going to change that.

We competed for the American Education Award for Art. I hoped doing so would give the kids something to feel good about. Sure enough, it did, and it made the teachers feel good, too. We won awards at just about every grade level. After several years, we'd won all kinds of awards. That gave a positive vibe to the teachers and the students.

I tried something a little different by getting some of the more outstanding teachers we had to roam around to some of the other classes to observe, retrain, or help the teachers who weren't doing well. They agreed to do that. That took place 30 years ago. Now they call them "resource teachers." I used my own staff. I also had teachers videotape each other and critique their lessons to improve instruction schoolwide.

I noticed some of my other teachers were excellent with the kids. Those teachers helped me figure out the best way to discipline the kids without paddling. When I was supposed to be paddling them, I'd hit the table, and say, "You better not do it again." Finally, they'd be crying, and I'd pat them on the butt and tell them to get out of there. Eventually, I didn't have kids getting sent to the office. You can't paddle kids today.

When some of my teachers said they didn't like noise in the cafeteria, I told them the noise level didn't bother me. After all, the kids needed to talk. That led me to take over in the cafeteria. I had a stoplight installed. When the light hit yellow, that meant it was getting a little too noisy.

There were a lot of gangs around Walter Bracken, which stood across the street from a low-income housing area. I would walk through that neighborhood to make visits to my students and their families. Some of their family members were in gangs. I would talk to parents and everybody got to know me. Most of them already knew my reputation before I got there. They just loved me coming around and visiting, conversing with them and assuring them that we'd be okay.

Probably 25 to 35 percent of our kids were homeless. I'd visit them in the homeless shelters. Talk to them. Because they knew we were a loving school, they always worked hard and we never had any issues.

I'd tell the parents if they were interested, they could come to school and go in the classroom at any time. My teachers were instructed to keep their doors unlocked to allow such visits.

I started a parent group. We had teachers who taught English to the Spanish-speaking parents.

Somebody came to the school selling memory tapes, which were supposed to help you improve your memory. Basically, it involved memorizing stuff through association. Anyway, they asked me to try it out. The guy told me that my students could learn how to remember things using numbers and images. Since I tried all kinds of stuff to elevate the kids' educations, I agreed to try it. Once I let him know that I thought the tapes worked, he asked me to do a commercial to help promote the benefits of the memory tool. I went on TV to do the commercials and said, "These memory tapes are fantastic."

Later, I found out that Alex Trebek had been the person I appeared with on the commercials. Of course, he went on to become a legend on the quiz show *Jeopardy!*

While I was at Walter Bracken, Judy and I decided to take real estate classes so we could get licensed. Judy wanted to do mental-health counseling, but hadn't gotten a job at that point, so real estate sounded like a good alternative. We both loved to go in and out of houses to look at them. We loved to look at new furniture, and how houses were set up to give us ideas for our home.

Las Vegas was growing like mad at the time. Once we got our licenses, I felt like selling real estate would be easy. I knew I could sell.

We joined the No. 1 company that sold houses in Law Vegas—we were quite impressed by the owner of the company. And once I began to sell, I confirmed my belief that selling houses would come easy to me.

I'd talk to people about a house and I'd show the house to them. I found selling the new homes particularly easy. You'd just show up and you didn't have to do any work, because the new home's salespeople gave you a percentage. So I sold real estate in the summers and on weekends. If you worked at an elementary school, you didn't work during the summer. So that became a nice supplemental income for me.

During that same time, Judy got pregnant. Once pregnant, she stopped working.

Based on my background, and how my family struggled with money when I was growing up, you would have thought that moving to a one-income family situation would have rattled me with anxiety about shouldering the financial load. It didn't. I thought we were in pretty good shape. Plus, Judy was able to assist with her savings.

I had two houses that I owned, which I rented. Because I was a go-getter. When I was first a teacher, I set my money aside in an annuity and I met a lady named Betty Ellison, who was a clerk at Eldorado High School. She advised me to buy land. I bought my first house with my income tax refund check when I was at Eldorado High. That was my second year of teaching. Not too long after that, I bought five acres. The income I got from those two investments eased my mind.

I continued to sell real estate and actually made the "Bronze Medallion Club," which was a big deal back then. Judy was shocked that I had closed over $1 million for the year and at all the new salespeople I'd beaten out. Even when promotions were held, I would beat out the others, whether it was selling the most for the week, having the most listings, or any number of things. I would win TV sets and all kinds of little prizes.

Judy and I experienced a big day when we welcomed our first child, Julie Denise, into the world on June 4, 1988.

Back in those days, we were huge fans of *The Cosby Show*. The show, which starred Bill Cosby, was the top-rated TV show in the country. We craved the few shows that starred a Black cast. Cosby starred in *I Spy* and Judy and I both remembered Diahann Carroll, who was the first Black woman to star in her own network show.

We just loved *The Cosby Show*—just ate it up. We wouldn't miss an episode. Sometimes we'd watch an episode twice. Being a religious family, we were so proud that there was a show that depicted a Black family with healthy values. We would talk about the show and wonder why more families didn't strive to be like the Huxtable family on that show.

We were so taken with *The Cosby Show* that we gave our daughter the middle name Denise, which was the name of the character on the show played by Lisa Bonet.

Julie's birth came the last week of 1987-1988 school. I got the notice that she might be going sooner than you think. When the time came, Judy waked me up in the middle of the night. I had to rush her to the hospital. Our daughter came prematurely, so that was a little scary, and Judy had to have a cesarean delivery.

Julie was beautiful from the first day and still is today. My friend John Bass—they later named a school after him—came over after she was born and I told him, "She's a genius, she's a genius. She's so smart." He used to tease me about that.

Because of my participation in helping to raise my brothers and sisters, I wasn't too panicked about becoming a father. Throughout the pregnancy, and after Julie's birth, Judy thought I acted too laid-back. And she didn't think I was doing my part. That kept her mad at me the whole time. She said I didn't help enough because I was too busy being a principal as a priority over the family.

Most nights, I came home totally exhausted, whether that exhaustion came from school or from participation in the multiple organizations to which I belonged. I can't even remember all of them that I served on, including stuff like registering people to vote for the NAACP. Going to all kinds of meetings. Judy felt overwhelmed with child care. I expected her to cook, and she resented that. I was going by the old mode for fatherhood as per my stepfather, Daddy Walt. That meant Judy was expected to take care of our daughter, wash the dishes, do the floors. She was thinking, "How come he doesn't come to the dishes? Doesn't he know I'm tired, too?"

In July of 1988, I attended a national conference on at-risk children in Oregon. That trip gave me the platform to tout the message that every student could learn if they had the proper instruction and encouragement.

Carolyn Reedom was also invited to the conference. She was the principal at McDoniel Elementary, which, like Walter Bracken, was in the Clark County School District. That conference was great, affording Carolyn and me the opportunity to swap ideas and success stories with those from other states.

I could not express myself enough that too many people identified at-risk children and expected them to fail. Like I told those at the conference, I constantly told my teaching staff that I did not expect any of them to fail at their jobs. Conversely, I also told them they should not expect any of their students to fail. My creed was that every child deserved to learn. That was the first thing. Second, they could learn. And, finally, at Walter Bracken, I stressed they would learn.

We had many experiences at Walter Bracken where at-risk students, who had done poorly, underwent complete changes. Those changes didn't necessarily translate to going from Fs to As, but they did show significant improvement.

Because our kids who were poor went on to achieve, Walter Bracken Elementary got recognized nationally for helping all kids in a welcoming environment. In line with the idea of achieving excellence at Walter Bracken, I made sure we registered to compete for the National Blue-Ribbon Schools Award.

The award was given annually to different schools in different states. Schools must compete locally, then statewide. After that, your state had to nominate you.

I'll never forget taking the time to fill out the paperwork for us to compete for that award. The application felt like a marathon session. It had to be double spaced, no more than so many pages, no errors, and all kinds of other stuff. And you had to have it in by the deadline. Because my secretary was sick, I ended up doing it by myself. I worked all day during the regular school day, then worked on the application after school until about 5 a.m. I went home to change clothes after that and took it to FedEx. I remember thinking that I should get some stock in FedEx, "it's a pretty good deal." I didn't follow my instincts, and I should have. FedEx has done pretty well.

After I sent the package that morning, I returned for another school day. Between completing the paperwork, and working at school, I worked 24 consecutive hours, then went back to work.

The award was graded on the following: visionary leadership; creating a sense of shared purpose among administrators, faculty, students, and parents; creating a climate conducive to effective teaching; and creating an environment that conveyed that children of all ability levels could learn.

Also included among the criteria were academic achievement and responsible behavior on the part of the students; a high degree of parental and community involvement; and a "can-do" attitude toward problem solving. It's based on the environment of the school, if it's a welcoming, learning environment. And that you're attending to all the kids in the school.

In February of 1990, Walter Bracken became just the second school in Clark County history to become one of the 197 finalists for the Elementary School Recognition Program. We did so out of 498 schools nationwide. The U.S. Department of Education administered the program. Prior to Walter Bracken Elementary qualifying as a finalist, Vegas Verdes Elementary had been the only school from the area to qualify.

On March 12, 1990, education officials visited the school and talked to students, parents, and teachers, then took that information back to the White House.

In early May of 1990, we received word that the U.S. Department of Education under George H.W. Bush had designated Walter Bracken as the first elementary school in Las Vegas as a "National Blue Ribbon School." Nationally, Walter Bracken Elementary was one of 221 "Blue Ribbon" elementary schools.

Upon receiving word that we'd won the award, the administration and faculty felt like, "Mission accomplished at Bracken." We were like, "We told you guys we could do this." I was really the one telling them all along that we could do it, because the teachers didn't really believe it.

I felt that if I could convince those teachers that they were winners, they could convince the kids. Because initially, they had been like, "Oh, we have the worst school." Teachers who don't want to teach are used to getting along and going along, like, "The kids can't do this, can't do that."

While outsiders might have been surprised at us receiving the recognition, nobody close to us would have. Insiders knew how tired we were and how hard we had worked on a daily basis. We were recognized because of all of my kids, whether they were low income, special ed, ethnicity, all of them were achieving at high levels and moving forward.

Across the country, the number of schools recognized depended on how many applied and how many met the national standards. One Las Vegas-area school that I'd stolen teachers from was flat out pissed at me because I understood the criteria that needed to be reached to get the award. They had twice tried to get the award and lost. And it was an excellent school. I'm not sure that school applied that particular year. Schools give up because it's so hard to meet all the requirements.

The *Las Vegas Review-Journal* quoted me as follows: "If it wasn't for the teachers who really care about all the kids here, we could not do it. They should have all the credit. I just got out of their way—most of the time."

I felt as though teamwork from the teachers, students, and parents earned us the award, as all personified our motto: "We care. We share. We work together."

The teachers I had were the best thing that happened to me. I can't tell you how fortunate I was to have had the best of the best.

Ten of my teachers at Walter Bracken would become principals during their careers.

I continued to attend conferences and training sessions—anything that had anything to do with developmental training. Whether it was NABSE or the district where they taught specific reading skills. I started one of the first pre-kindergarten too. We did anything to help the kids. It just elevated them. We were recognized by the Nevada State Department of Education for having improved the Chapter I students' reading scores the most in the state.

My supervisor trained some of the educators in Saudi Arabia before he came to Las Vegas. An excellent writer, specific and detail oriented, he demanded that I strive for excellence. I give him credit for making me as good as I became with writing evaluations. Even though I believed he really didn't think I would be able to handle the pressures he placed on me.

If you put a teacher on notice, you had to bring in at least two principals, and there was a long document chronicling all the deficiencies of the teacher. And my supervisor told me I had to do that with one of my teachers. In the meantime, I had another teacher with some discipline issues, so I was writing her up. Then I learned that the union would not take these charges lightly.

I had a hard time with the union because I had a low rating with the teachers. That's what happens when you write them up left and right for everything. The union stayed on my case, making me out to be the worst principal ever, and that I was incompetent. After all that was done, and we cleaned the place up, the union later endorsed me to run for office.

I learned you just couldn't take the stuff personally. That was the union representative's job. Our district personnel administrator, Eva Simmons, told me that and continued to teach me how to deal with teacher unions.

In my five years as principal at Walter Bracken, I learned that I couldn't get everything implemented at once. I tried everything from the parents getting involved to having teams at the school and having the teachers surveyed. I worked on those teacher ratings. I worked on the things that they had been ranked low on for a long time until I got higher ratings. I made sure that I frequented the classrooms a lot, and that the instruction was child centered, not teacher centered. All of those effective school principles.

The achievements we made at Walter Bracken prompted an offer for me to take over a new school, and I accepted the offer to move on to Robert Lunt Elementary.

## CHAPTER ELEVEN

My offer to go to Robert Lunt Elementary came during the winter of 1990. Lunt would be one of the 13 new schools opening in Las Vegas in the fall of 1990. That number of new schools was the most ever opened in the area in one year.

Anticipation and excitement by everybody at the school accompanied our anticipation for the opening of Lunt. We'd been getting everything up and running, and we expected to be on the front page of the newspapers and featured on TV once we finally opened. Unfortunately, that didn't happen. Because tragedy struck my old school.

On August 26, 1990, a 15-year-old sophomore at Eldorado High shot and killed a 16-year-old junior in the school's cafeteria.

Having roamed the halls of Eldorado earlier in my career, that incident really hit home for me.

The shooter had been an ROTC member at Eldorado, and a respectable kid. He did not have a criminal record. Like other incidents of that nature that occurred before and after, nobody could foresee the shooter doing anything like what he did that day. Everyone at the school, and in the community, was numb and felt vulnerable. We all handled that news as best we could. In the end, we were left to deal with a sad chapter for the area, and a precursor for inexplicable future events in the United States.

Two happier notes also came that fall. The first came the day after the tragedy.

My wife and I were expecting our second child. Judy had almost reached full-term when she kept her scheduled August 27, 1990, appointment with her gynecologist. However, the baby wasn't due for another month. To her surprise, the doctor told her she had gone into labor, which prompted a cesarean delivery.

Judy wasn't thrilled about the doctor's decision that she needed to be cut on again. A part of her felt like the doctor had made the call to deliver in order to meet the doctor's vacation schedule.

Jasmine Michelle Hamilton was born five weeks early. Despite her premature arrival, there were no health issues. She came into the world with an inherit toughness, packaged with a sense of confidence. From day one, she wore an expression of wonder, and she's managed to maintain that ever since. We were blessed to have a second child.

The other happy note that fall stemmed from the National Blue Ribbon Schools Award we'd won at Bracken.

Though I'd moved from Bracken Elementary to Lunt, I went to Washington, D.C., for the ceremony in September of 1990. Two of my teachers from Bracken accompanied me on the trip, Mrs. Freddie Bevill and Mrs. Mary Wiser. What an occasion!

We found ourselves in the Rose Garden at the White House. George H.W. Bush spoke that day, and Barbara Bush even walked over to me and said hello. I remember finding myself just chitchatting away with the First Lady. What an honor. She was a class act. I ended up getting a nice photograph shot with her. Reflecting on all the work that the Blue Ribbon Schools Award represented made the day more special. We had great teamwork at Bracken, and had worked together to achieve a goal. All kinds of lessons could be learned from that, specifically the rewards that are possible through effort.

Walter Bracken Elementary received a big flag that recognized its achievement. The school got listed in different publications that touted the school for being among the best in the United States. The Nevada state department had already made a big deal about the school being one of the top schools in the state. The national recognition added icing to the cake. The credit should have gone more to the teachers. We had a fabulous team at Bracken School: Mrs. Ola Holliway, Mrs. Debbie Powell, Ms. Linda Gipson, Ms. Otha Roberson, Mr. Carl Dawson, and Mrs. Carlis Arnold.

Moving on to Lunt Elementary delivered me into a new climate, along with a new work environment.

Prior to heading to the new school, I learned I would be allowed to take along with me half of my staff from Walter Bracken. Those teachers who left with me were on an emotional high from all the success we'd had. After what we'd done at Bracken, I told my teachers that Lunt would be a piece of cake. And sure enough, my words were prophetic.

Because I had organized the teachers to run the school when they were at Bracken, they had the blueprint for what needed to be done at the new school, and they did a great job of following that blueprint. To ensure every child could read and do math, I arranged for two staff to function as resource teachers, one for math and the other for language arts. Their mission was to keep tabs on every teacher in the school to make sure they taught the kids as well as they could.

My reputation preceded my arrival to the largely Hispanic community where Robert Lunt Elementary sat. The parents loved me, particularly the Hispanic parents. They are very caring. When they adopt you as part of their family, you're in. Gangs were prevalent in the area, but I never had a problem with gangs, which I attributed largely to having some credibility when I assumed the position.

We had everything in place to ensure a quality education for any kid in the school. The kids just fell into line. If you have high expectations, good discipline, order, and strategies, you're going to have success.

Just as we did at Bracken, we had an open contract in which we said, "Here are the things we're going to do, and we guarantee you as a staff that we're going to get these things done." We went so far as to put up a sign on the school door that read, "We guarantee every kid will attain high achievement."

My boss told me, "I don't think you should guarantee anything." Like we were writing checks we couldn't cover. I told him, "Oh, no. We guarantee it."

I'll acknowledge that such a guarantee might have sounded overly ambitious. But based on what we'd accomplished in the past, we knew we could guarantee the results we were going to get. Along with that guarantee came expectations for the parents. We—the teachers and staff at the school—told them we were holding them accountable for a list of things we expected from them. And we had them sign off on that list. That created a contract. We stuck to our end of the bargain, and we held them accountable to keeping their end as well. That had been a tried-and-true method at Bracken, and that method worked again at Lunt. My staff and I simply had to follow the formula we'd created. Sometimes you don't have to reinvent the wheel.

Basically, all I had to do at Lunt was retrain the new secretary, and make sure the right books were ordered. I'd been a micro "hands-on" guy at Bracken and suddenly I'd become a macro "big-picture" guy at Lunt. What I didn't envision about moving to the new school was finding myself bored stiff.

Dealing with that boredom, I threw myself into a lot of the activities away from the school. I'd always been involved in such activities away from the school, anyway, and the activities that I got involved with were ones that impacted the school.

NABSE continued to hold a great interest for me. Being passionate about the organization that had impacted me so, I dove into the deep end of the pool, getting more heavily involved. As president of LVABSE (Las Vegas Alliance of Black School Educators), I attended NABSE's national conference. I went to regional conferences, too. There were times when I would present about the things we were doing in Las Vegas, and the other presidents would present what they were doing. Sharing notes is a great way to learn.

In addition to serving as the LVABSE president, I held many different offices for many different organizations. To name a couple,

I served as the Las Vegas president of the NAACP, and I served as president of a new organization I founded, which is still going strong, B-CON—Black Community Organization Network.

My motivation for starting B-CON came from a desire to find a way to honor the best and the brightest African American students. Thus, I contacted several organizations and welcomed them to work together to try and reach that goal at a discussion meeting I convened.

My friend and mentor, Jim Pughsley, represented Kappa Alpha Psi; Margaret Crawford represented Alpha Kappa Alpha; Eva Simmons and Joann Pughsley, Delta Sigma Theta; and Lois Ice represented the Links. We accepted the name B-CON, which, we agreed, represented a beacon of light for the future. Others were founding members after we held follow-up meetings to make the organization official. Going forward, we held an annual ceremony to honor exceptional African American students based on their achievement. In addition to honoring exceptional students, B-CON also motivated others to do well. The organization helped provide scholarship and counseling assistance, creating possibilities for students to attend college, who might not otherwise have been able to do so.

Because I'd always believed in continuing education, I have always pushed my teachers to do everything possible to improve themselves. Accordingly, I supported my teachers by attending many of the conferences I'd pushed my teachers to attend. Where professional development was concerned, I'd been taught to be aware of whatever my teachers were being taught. Following that sentiment, I felt strongly that I needed that familiarity in order to help support them when they were implementing new ideas. NABSE's weren't the only conferences I pushed. Countless other conferences were available to broaden one's horizons. My teachers gathered a lot of quality information for professional development by attending those conferences, as did I.

Among those conferences was one held by the International Reading Association, where a speaker presented information to the want-to-be principals in the audience. I have no idea how many of my teachers were there that day, but like always, I wanted to stay informed about what they were being told. Since I'd never been content to just be a fly on the wall, I asked questions at that IRA conference. Then, during a break, I stepped outside and a young lady approached me. She proceeded to question me about the presentation that had just taken place. Her name was Glenda Hildreth and she was from Rockford, Illinois. Later she asked me if I'd mind if she arranged for a friend of hers, Rosalyn Walker (Rockford's personnel director), to give me a call, adding, "All kinds of things are happening in Rockford that you might be interested in."

I told her I'd be happy to talk to her friend.

Hildreth's friend turned out to be the Rockford school district's personnel director, who contacted me shortly thereafter. She informed me that they had an open assistant superintendent position and they wanted me to apply. She told me that I would be a good fit for the position.

I applied and the next thing I knew the process began.

During one of the interviews that followed, they told me I had great experience as a principal and asked if I would accept a director's position.

I wasn't biting on that. "No, I'm not going to go for director. I could probably do that in Las Vegas. But the assistant superintendent, I'd be interested in that."

Even though they cited my lack of experience, I felt confident in my ability and qualifications. I had already worked at the central office in Las Vegas. I hadn't held the title of assistant superintendent, but my work there did allow me to experience what it was like to work with a hundred schools at a time.

Obviously, I cleared the first hurdle of the interview process, because the superintendent, Dr. Maurice Sullivan, flew out to Las Vegas to see me. Our meeting took place at Lunt Elementary.

160

Everything at Lunt was sparkling and new, which made quite an impression on Sullivan. To say that he was overwhelmed by the trappings of my office—and my job—would be an understatement. My office had more than just a desk. I had a huge conference room, a TV, and all the latest stuff. They even equipped me with a cellphone, which wasn't a standard piece of equipment back then. Further, Sullivan's eyes nearly popped out when he saw that the school had Apple computers. At one point he told me, "What a setup! Why would you want to leave this?"

Afterward, I felt good about Sullivan's visit, and my instincts were right. He had liked enough of what he saw to extend me an invitation to meet with him two weeks later at the O'Hare Airport Hyatt in Chicago. That fueled my optimism that they wanted to hire me. I figured the job was mine to lose. That put me in a state of mind where I wanted to cross all the T's and dot all the I's—I didn't want to fumble the ball and blow the opportunity. Believing that failing to prepare would be preparing to fail, I did my best to prepare for that meeting.

I hired a service to clean up my resume, and, for the first time in my life, I even had my nails done. While I felt kind of stupid about having my nails done, I wanted to make sure nothing about me would be seen as a detriment.

Sullivan drank hard liquor during the interview. I wasn't much of a drinker, so I only sipped a glass of water while I answered his questions with caution. I watched him thumb through my resume—back and forth, back and forth—and I thought, "Must be a good resume. Thank goodness I had someone look at it." I'm not sure if he ever noticed my nails.

The interview lasted about 90 minutes. I felt good about the way it had gone. Sullivan said he would get back to me. I knew they'd be offering me the job.

The Rockford opportunity appealed to me for several reasons.

First, I had some concerns about getting blackballed if I remained in Las Vegas. I had been involved in a lawsuit.

The local Las Vegas NABSE group—Las Vegas Alliance of Black School Educators (LVABSE) sued the school district after the board of trustees purged the Clark County School District of virtually all its top-ranking Black administrators in the spring of 1989. The federal civil rights lawsuit accused the Clark County School District of racial discrimination and sought to set aside an administrative reorganization thought to be unfair to Blacks. Further, the lawsuit maintained that the district denied equal employment opportunities to Blacks, denied them promotions, and alleged that Blacks were transferred on a discriminatory basis.

The climate of the city wasn't toxic. But in the school district, a tense climate existed. Different groups—Hispanic, Black, White, and Jewish—were trying to vie for control of the school district. That resulted in a fight for who would have the most control of the school district. And they wanted to wrestle it out of the hands of the Blacks, which, eventually, they were successful in doing.

Daisey Miller, the president of the LVABSE, was ready to go downtown to agree to sue the school district for discrimination against personnel and also not attending to the needs of the Black kids. At that same time, they had asked some of us to go and meet with the national NABSE, to ask for advice. I was vice president of LVABSE at the time, and Daisey ended up having me sign the document to sue. Accordingly, I felt the pressure of any possible repercussions from being associated with that suit. Those of us involved with the lawsuit believed that we would be blackballed, and that none of us would ever be promoted again.

Primarily, the Rockford job appealed to me professionally. Continuing to be upwardly mobile would be good for my career.

Family added to the attractiveness of the Rockford job.

The idea of moving sounded good to Judy. Moving close to her twin sisters, Marcia and Monica, sounded even more appealing. Both lived near Chicago.

Marcia and Monica are younger than Judy, who is close to all seven of her siblings.

Judy also liked that I'd be getting a promotion. She liked ambition, too. Getting the job in Rockford would demonstrate ambition, that I wanted to continue advancing on my professional career path.

Judy and I were pleased when Sullivan called shortly after the Chicago interview to offer me the job. I accepted.

Since I began at Lunt in the fall of 1990 and had moved to Rockford by March of 1991, I obviously did not spend a great deal of time at the new school. However, I felt proud about what we accomplished at the school on my watch.

My main accomplishment had been getting half of the staff from Bracken to transfer. They brought all the procedures and protocols we had set up at Bracken, so Lunt became a fine machine from the beginning.

## CHAPTER TWELVE

Becoming the assistant superintendent of instruction for the
Rockford School District really got me excited. Getting moved up
from principal to assistant superintendent was unprecedented. Not
only did I consider the move an achievement, I also considered it to
be a remarkable opportunity.

I've always had a "save the world" complex. I believe my
attitude or state of mind can be attributed to my Bible study. I
always wanted to be Samson, Jesus, or Moses—I wanted to save the
world! I couldn't wait to get busy in Rockford. I like to be involved
in stuff.

While I recognized I'd had a cushy job at Lunt, and for sure,
a lot of people would have been content to have my position, I
wanted more. All I could think was, "This is not great, I have a lot
of work yet to do in my life." I wanted to get to Washington, D.C.,
and work in the White House. I wanted to help the country. I wanted
to do my part.

From the travel I'd done, and from all my reading, I was
aware there were plenty of kids in need. I wanted to help those kids
in the United States. I wanted to help those kids throughout the
world. I'd always thought more globally than just Las Vegas, or
Alabama, or whatever city I lived in at the time. In order for our kids

to do a lot better, good leaders were needed. That could be narrowed down to the need of having good, moral people with a lot of integrity to help guide the policies. I wanted to make an impact.

I knew from the work I'd done at Bracken, and from how we'd carried out that same plan at Lunt, that success could be had at every school. Everybody just needed to do more. I needed to lead the effort to do more.

Having been in the Las Vegas school system's central office, I knew how large the school system was and which schools needed help. I'd thought, "Gosh, I wish I could go back to the central office." That's where I felt I could help most. But a lot of competition existed for those spots. A very political environment existed. In contrast, the Rockford position made me the assistant superintendent over everything—meaning I would be the top assistant superintendent, directly under the superintendent. I'd be over all of the elementary schools. Over all the high schools. All the special education departments. All the professional development. All the student assignment—where kids would go. All the magnet schools. And, even though I wasn't the assistant superintendent of the budget, I would be the main person directing where the money went. All of that was pretty enticing, essentially because the job put me in a position to effect change.

There were noticeable strengths and weaknesses I recognized upon my arrival to Rockford. A strength came in the fact so many different groups of people wanted to make a positive difference. The district had some excellent teachers, administrators, and a community that wanted better schools. The weakness came in the fact school leaders had rarely included the groups that were different from the majority. For some reason, messages from other groups had been shut out and there had not been enough inclusion of the disenfranchised groups.

Rockford definitely had challenges, including issues with outsiders, which is not unusual for school districts. Understandably, they were skeptical of me before I arrived.

I'd always enjoyed insider status in Las Vegas. In Rockford, I found myself in a different role. Not only was I an outsider when I arrived, I'd been slotted just below the superintendent. Resentment and a lot of whispers followed.

Rockford had enjoyed a booming furniture industry in the 1880s before evolving into an industrial area that revolved around machine tools, heavy machinery, and the like. Of note, they were the home of the Rockford Peaches of the All-American Girls Professional Baseball League, which existed from 1944 through 1954. The Peaches were one of the teams featured in the 1992 movie starring Tom Hanks, *A League of Their Own*.

Despite Rockford's history as a manufacturing Mecca, the city began to experience financial struggles somewhere along the way. That resulted in a district-wide budget crisis. An offshoot of that crisis brought the threat of all athletic programs getting shut down. You can cut a lot of things out of any school budget without drawing much attention. Athletics is not one of those things. Like most places in the country, Rockford liked its athletics and didn't want to see anything happen to them. Particularly as a line item deleted to meet some school budget.

However, before that happened, Dr. Sullivan worked with the Rockford Sports Coalition to find a solution, which they did, and the games played on. I think he earned a lot of points in the community for finding a solution.

Sports wasn't the only problem.

Prior to my hiring, some citizens alleged that the school district had established different outcomes for the Black children, and had discriminated against the Black schools. Thirteen schools on one side of the tracks were segregated. Those schools got the low end of what was being offered to students, including inadequate supplies, upkept schools, and the overall quality of their education. For example, those schools were not allowed to have AP classes. Students at those schools weren't provided the same access to education that would lead to graduating with the possibility of going to college. Lots and lots of things led to the lawsuit against the Rockford Board of Education that was filed on May 11, 1989.

"People Who Care" were the plaintiffs in the case that attacked the 1989 Reorganization Plan that had been adopted by the defendant, the Rockford Board of Education School District. In addition to attacking the Reorganization Plan, the suit also charged the district with decades of discrimination against minorities. According to U.S. Magistrate Judge P. Michael Mahoney, the Rockford School District had for decades been guilty of both intentional abuse and benign neglect in class assignments, district leadership, busing, and facilities.

The suit did no go well for the Rockford Board of Education.

For example, when they began bringing in superintendents, consultants, and the like to the court, to discuss the merits of the lawsuit, one superintendent told the court that one of the board members referred to staff and students as "niggers"—just openly used that term. I found that astonishing.

Skepticism existed in both the Black and White communities.

Black communities were skeptical because things never seemed to improve. White communities were skeptical because "This Maurice Sullivan, this White guy from Wisconsin, is going to try and tell us how to handle our integration issues? Then the court is going to make him hire Black folks."

Dr. Sullivan took a stance and said, "We're going to help integrate this place."

Dr. Eugene Eubanks, a NABSE icon, was appointed by the federal court to oversee implementation of an anti-discriminatory school improvement program. Court-appointed lawyers and Dr. Eubanks—the court master—would dictate much of what would follow. NABSE held him in high regard, and he would become instrumental in a lot of what happened during my time at Rockford. I respected him a great deal.

Dr. Eubanks basically controlled the school board through the lost court case. He'd been the guy who asked the difficult questions on behalf of the lawsuit people—"People Who Care"—and the court, which had taken over the district. Questions like, "What are you doing about differentiating instruction, bringing in mentors, and integrating your staff?"

The case resulted in Sullivan trying to find a high-level Black candidate for his Superintendent's Leadership Cabinet and he found yours truly. That made me the first Black person to be hired at such a high level they'd ever had.

Since the board had been found guilty of discrimination, the court took over and the board had to do what the court said. The court did allow that the board could have input, but the final say would be based on what was brought out through those meetings with Dr. Eubanks, who became the real superintendent. Sullivan and Eubanks actually worked well together to get things done.

A lot of the direction for my duties stemmed from the agreement with the courts and all the lawyers.

The lawyers and the superintendent met with the superintendent's cabinet level, mainly me and the other assistant superintendents. We would talk about what needed to occur. Then I would go back and talk to my staff, which covered the whole district. We'd discuss how we planned to implement the lofty goals that were articulated in the meetings.

Even though the duties of my new position swamped me, the driving mission of NABSE was constantly providing me with direction and focus. I constantly met with the many consultants, prompting several meetings every day of the week. On Monday, the superintendent would meet with me and his cabinet and four lawyers. That would eat up most of the day. Afterward, we'd rehash everything until 10 o'clock or 11 that same night. Tuesday, I'd meet with the superintendent's staff. We'd talk about what we just talked about with all of those lawyers. Wednesdays, I'd meet with my educational staff. Thursdays would be the union meetings. Fridays, I'd try to catch up on work. I would work until 10 o'clock or 11 every night.

The public wasn't happy with many of the changes being made in the school system. Most were upset about property taxes being raised every year while property values continued to spiral down. We were charged with spending $30 million a year on the 15 Black schools, or the "schools across the river." That infusion included everything from renovation to professional development, training teachers and principals, hiring new people for all kinds of positions.

Elsewhere in the $130 million budget, $15 million a year needed to be cut from the other 15 to 20 schools in the district, due to the lack of taxes. Dr. Sullivan gave me the responsibility of having the final say on all funds—either spend or cut. Word got out in the community, creating a challenging situation. Eventually, I had to cut down some of the kindergartens. That triggered an interesting late-night situation.

Like a lot of nights in Rockford, the weather was freezing— Rockford would regularly drop below zero. Judy and I were in bed when we heard a knock at the front door. When I opened the door, a lady stood on the doorstep and let me have it. "You cut my kindergarten teacher! I want to know why you cut my kindergarten teacher! My kid doesn't have a kindergarten teacher!" I'm like, "Can we talk about this later? It's too cold, ma'am."

During this period, Asa Hilliard, a professor of Urban Education at Georgia State University, grew to have a big influence on me. Not only did he have a voice at NABSE, he'd also been responsible for the "African/African-American Baseline Essays," which were educational materials he'd compiled for the Portland public school district in Portland, Oregon. According to the "Preface to the African/African-American Baseline Essays" their purpose was to "provide information about the history, culture, and contributions of Africans and African-Americans in the disciplines of Art, Language Arts, Mathematics, Science, Social Studies, and Music."

When I'd been the principal at Bracken, I had gone to a conference in Portland, Oregon, to work with the Tom Peters group. Peters had written the book *In Search of Excellence*. He and his company were employed by Ron Herndon, the director of the Albina Head Start School in Portland, where they were actively trying to increase achievement for the kids. Principals from all over the country were invited to that conference and I'd been lucky enough to be one of those principals. Later I discovered that Portland had also invited Hilliard to identify a way to diversify the curriculum for their schools.

The idea was to come up with a curriculum that taught within the cultures of many minorities, infusing into the curriculum those cultures and histories. Later, I implemented that plan into our teaching at Bracken.

At Rockford, I promoted that same design, and then the team jumped in and helped ensure we diversified the curriculum. The lawyers agreed with the themes and the court agreed to it. Later, the board agreed and we were off with including more details. I also made a presentation to all the district administrators, the central office, and the principals in which I touted the Ron Edmonds correlates of effective schools, the ones that I used to build Bracken. The idea that every kid could learn at a high level was still relatively new.

During that full-blown presentation—complete with overheads—I reviewed those correlates. Afterward, Sullivan expressed how pleased and impressed he had been with my presentation. That presentation caught the attention of a lot of administrators about where I wanted the district to go while also satisfying the court, which had to find my idea equitable. I said, "If you want to see equity, this is how you do it."

I instituted assistant principals throughout the district and I said we were going to diversify them by trying to get as many

African American and minority principals as possible. Mostly
African American, because they didn't have too many Hispanics.

My efforts provided the first opportunity for the school
district to infuse diversity, because they didn't have hardly any
Blacks working in important positions within the district. That had
been one of the criticisms by the folks who brought the complaint to
the district.

Accomplishing said tasks gave me a great deal of satisfaction and
allowed me to feel as though I was performing well in my new job. I
had gone from having little to do at Lunt to being stretched to the
limit in Rockford. As always, I continued to take on more.

When the district lost a curriculum director early in my
tenure, the position wasn't filled. Instead, I assumed those duties by
becoming the curriculum director. That proved to be a good turn of
events for me because I didn't have any experience as a curriculum
director.

I had taken courses in curriculum, so I knew it was a
different animal, because it's all academic—using that cranium of
yours. I had to review what the course of studies were for each
school.

In one of those all-day lawyer sessions, Dr. Eubanks had
come up with "You need to try to accommodate both sides of the

river, the Whites and the Blacks, to see if we can get a school that will be very diverse, and one where you accommodate the high level, low level, the Whites and Blacks." Normally that falls to a magnet school. He concluded, "You need to come up with a magnet school. Hamilton, since you're the curriculum person, I guess you're going to be designing it."

They wanted to build a new school, and I had to come up with a theme for the school. I also had to design the school's curriculum.

I'd always loved social studies, and I loved learning about cultures, so I suggested creating a global studies magnet school. I wrote an outline for what I thought should be in the curriculum, which included a lot of social studies and multicultural learning.

Lewis Lemon High School was born. After its opening, that school produced the highest test scores in the state for years.

While I found much of my work rewarding, that did not include all the meetings dealing with the court. That's why I found myself caught in somewhat of a bittersweet situation.

Like always, I couldn't have enough involvement. They didn't have an NAACP ACTSO (Academic, Cultural, Technical, Scientific Olympics) in Rockford, so I found a coordinator for the program and started one.

We got the kids to compete in different areas. When kids accomplish something, their reactions and emotions are quite rewarding. The community appreciated my efforts, too. When I went to church, they made me feel like a rock star. The pastor would stop everything and say, "Dr. Hamilton and his family are here." Everybody would turn, because it was like, "Somebody has finally come to rescue us."

The Black folks in the community were appreciative of my efforts. Plenty of the White folks shared that feeling, too. They felt as though the time had come to create equity.

Because I wanted to maintain my blistering pace at work, I decided I needed to get myself into shape. The physical piece of one's being is as critical as the mental piece for the overall picture. I started getting up at 4:30 in the morning and driving to a YMCA located a half a mile from my work. I'd actually get there and wait in my car until they opened at 5 a.m. I'd always be one of the first to arrive. I'd do my workout—whether it was running, swimming, weights, elliptical, or whatever, then get to work about 6:30 a.m. That became my routine at Rockford for three years.

We bought a house located in an upper-class, White neighborhood in Rockford. We never really felt totally welcome there. Some of the neighbors would look at us like, "What are you doing here?" And we'd be like, "Because we can afford it here."

Judy still talks about one of our neighbor's houses that backed up to ours with no fence separating our backyards. She remembered the situation by recalling of our neighbor, "You know that lady never did speak to us. As many times as we had the kids out there, she would turn around, go back into her house, and slam her door."

I told Judy, "Well, some people are just like that."

We had other neighbors who were very nice.

The house we bought in Rockford was only two years old and easily the best house we'd ever lived in, before or after. Unfortunately, I rarely saw my family during the week. It was almost like they weren't there. But we did have the weekends together. While we didn't do a lot on weekends, we did have that time together. The kids were young, and we attended church regularly, so that helped a lot. Because we lived in cold weather for much of the year, we couldn't leave the house too much. We enrolled Julie in dance classes. Jasmine was too small to do much of anything. I did a lot of snow shoveling, and I helped build a lot of snowmen with the girls. Still, having family time only on the weekends, and not during the week, created a problem. Later, I would realize that I had been neglecting the family and leaving Judy with the little ones too much during my career.

Given what Judy had experienced growing up in West Point, Mississippi, she had already lived that "I'm going to help the city by sacrificing my kids." She had been sacrificed. For five straight years at elementary school, she played in the dirt with a stick, and ate by herself from the second grade through the sixth to help integrate the West Point, Mississippi, schools. She knew more than most what sacrifice felt like.

Judy began to resent me for giving too much at work and too little at home.

In fairness to her, she'd never really been that familiar with my duties and activities during my years as a principal in Las Vegas. She'd just seen me working day and night—when I got home from work, I'd retire to my office to do evaluations and all kinds of other things that needed to get done. I felt bad, but I don't think she realized how exhausted I was from all of the stuff I had to do for my job—I was really busy.

The situation only got worse in Rockford.

Judy grew resentful of me for not helping with the housework. This was especially hurtful, since she had worked outside of the house most of the years of our marriage, even after the children were born. Later, she told me she'd considered divorcing me. Again, I don't think she appreciated my situation and the stress that accompanied my job, nor did she understand how hard it was to come home and help with anything.

Once we finally discussed the matter, she told me that she'd had a role model growing up. Her father had helped around the house a lot until he experienced some issues toward the end of his life, like getting beat up for being a member of the NAACP. In her father, she had seen a male role model help her mother quite a bit. To that, I told her I did not have a role model. Neither my father, nor stepfather, helped with anything around the house. Those two believed women were supposed to cook and clean and do all of that. Of course, Judy didn't appreciate that. My behavior was what you would expect from an old military kind of husband. I later got it through my thick head that the way I'd acted had not been right. But at the time, I didn't know I was behaving badly. Once Judy began to spell out the situation, I felt bad about it.

Meanwhile, everything that happened at work in Rockford played out publicly in the media.

Almost every day, if I wasn't being interviewed by the newspaper or the radio, they reported on Dr. Sullivan. They talked about the superintendent like he was a dog. At one point, they accused him of having an affair with the lady I had replaced as the assistant superintendent. And they talked about how we were spending the money, then cutting programs. On the radio they'd say, "They're spending money on this and this. We're going to call Hamilton right now."

I did a lot of radio interviews via the telephone. I felt as though I was considerate and generous with my time. But what I gave never seemed to be enough. There were times when they called me when I was having quality time with my family. I'd say, "Can we talk later?" That would lead to them telling their audience, "Hamilton doesn't want to talk with us."

While I ranked as the highest superintendent in the district, there were two other assistant superintendents, one over finance and the other, William (Bill) Bowen, who was over operations (buses as well as personnel). Bowen was friends with the spokesperson for the lawsuit that had taken place. That spokesperson, who was Black, wanted Bowen to be the superintendent. Dr. Sullivan did not seem to trust Bowen, but the board did. Bowen often talked favorably about the merits of the lawsuit. The board didn't care for Dr. Sullivan, even though they had hired him and he went along with everything the court said.

Bowen tried to play both sides of the fence, but he always made sure the board knew that he was their boy. I felt he tried to undermine a lot of what the superintendent did.

After I'd been on the job eight months, Dr. Sullivan either got fired or resigned—I've never been sure what happened. A lot of people began telling me I needed to try and become the superintendent. Along with that narrative, some advised me to make sure I'd taken the test that would qualify me for the job. Further, they noted that taking the test early would be best, telling me, "Even if you're not going to become the superintendent, you need to be certified, because they're going to start kicking people out of their jobs if they're not certified."

Since I'd always been good at taking tests, I didn't fret. I simply took the necessary tests for proper certification and passed them. Then, when the time came for the empty superintendent's chair to be filled, I was the only person in the school district that had the qualifications to be certified as the superintendent.

Bowen badly wanted to be superintendent and had solid connections in the Illinois legislation, but he lacked the necessary qualifications. Rather than take the necessary certification tests, I believed he tried to use his legislation connections to get qualified. In the end, the state would not sign off on the waiver he sought that would have allowed him to become the superintendent.

Somebody had to be selected to fill Dr. Sullivan's vacant slot, and I became the choice. They offered me the position of interim superintendent. Though I didn't want the job, I listened to

Dr. Eubanks's advice when he told me, "Bernard, you should take it."

I asked him, "Why? I don't want to be involved in all this mess."

Dr. Eubanks had given the decision considerable thought and he promptly told me, "Just take the money. They're probably going to let Bill Bowen make most of the decisions, so you're just going to have to figure it out. You can work it out together. He can be the CEO and you're the superintendent. You just have to sign off on the paperwork."

Reluctantly, I took the job in October of 1992, leaving me as the interim superintendent before the end of my first year in Rockford. After the announcement of my new position, Bowen visited me. Just as Dr. Eubanks predicted, Bowen told me we'd attend board meetings and make decisions together.

Despite the interim title, I technically was the district superintendent. Nothing could be approved unless I signed off on it. I tried not to get involved in controversial decisions, and I wanted to avoid any internal fighting on the board.

My temporary assignment was only supposed to last eight months. By the end of that time period, they were supposed to have hired a full-time superintendent. Despite having temporary status, I set the following goals:

Improve finances; get parents, teachers, and administrators to speak with one voice; change the perception that things couldn't get better in Rockford schools; eliminate the perception that all children couldn't learn; and get more minority groups involved, and give them more reasons to believe their ideas counted.

I met quite a bit with "The Five White Rich Men," as they were called in the newspapers. That group had definite opinions about how the school district should be run, and how much smoother the district would run through their community outreach people. They also felt they could integrate the district a little smoother in relation to the court's decisions.

The board expanded from one to two Black members, and I did a lot of meeting with them, strategizing and trying to help them learn things. I served on many committees. All of them were out in the dark and sought more information on the district's intentions, or how they could get something done.

Bowen led the charge to find a permanent superintendent. I believed he wanted me out for the simple fact he still harbored designs on becoming superintendent and having all the power that came with the position. Even though Bowen served in a CEO-type role, he considered me a threat and felt as though I reduced his power. I wouldn't go along with stuff that wasn't by the book. I read everything thoroughly before I signed off on it.

Though I battled trying circumstances daily, I continued to try and fight for change.

For example, my efforts to improve the situation with AP classes. When I talked to the parents at a community group, I asked them, "Why are you against infusing, and making sure some of the Black kids get AP classes?" They said they didn't have anything against the Black kids, they just didn't think there was enough pie for everybody. If the Black kids started to take AP classes, they were "going to start getting some of our scholarships and we don't like that." Peel away the top soil and the reality was more like, "We want to keep our privilege."

The court was clear about this. It would not put up with the high schools and middle schools not allowing their minority kids to take AP and honors classes. That remained a hot button throughout my time in Rockford. Parents continued to complain that their kids might lose out on AP classes because we were going to force the integration of that.

Part of our summer training stressed that AP could be taught to anyone. Some of the principals didn't like that I took the stance that they weren't going to go along with the plan. That reluctance prompted me to fire ten principals and I had to rehire new ones. Firing those principals created a mound of paperwork, but I felt the action to fire those guys had to take place.

I believe I accomplished something through that episode, because I had to have the courage to execute the firings, I had to take the heat, and I had to do the work. Those firings created more work with the interview process to find new principals that followed.

I'm so hyper that the hours I kept in Rockford never brought me down. I always thought I could do more. I loved it. Getting up at 4:30 every morning, I couldn't wait to get to the YMCA, then getting to work, I thought that was exciting. I am sure Judy didn't think much of those hours.

Bowen's recommendation influenced the board to hire another assistant superintendent. The guy supposedly had experience as a superintendent. I believed Bowen wanted a puppet he could control and he believed he could use the guy to push me out of the job. The new guy had doctorates in Jesuit studies and in education. Despite those designations, he had a weak resume with questionable qualifications. I smelled something fishy. He just didn't sound legitimate, particularly when he said stuff you just wouldn't say if you'd been through a doctorate program. Later this man would be exposed for not having the credentials. He didn't have a doctorate in anything.

I'll give the man this: he could talk.

Eventually, the new guy told me there wasn't room for both of us. I told him he didn't have to worry about me, I intended to leave.

He left me alone after that.

By the start of my second year in Rockford, I began looking for an exit strategy. During that same period, Judy was pregnant with our third child.

Because her two previous deliveries had been cesarean, the doctors wanted to try and facilitate a natural birth. They deemed that another cesarean delivery would have put the baby and her at risk. The doctor ordered almost nine months of bed rest. Fortunately, I made enough to hire a full-time nanny to take care of the girls. That was a rough period.

Judy had a team of three to five doctors in Rockford monitoring her status. She had some electrical thing taped around her stomach and people in Atlanta were monitoring her. Atlanta had the equipment and the computers. We experienced a couple of scary experiences in the middle of the night when we had to rush to the hospital.

Judy ended up having her first natural delivery. We'd both prayed for a boy. And that's what we got. Bernard Steven Hamilton III was born May 26, 1993. I actually helped pull out his head during the delivery. He kept that beautiful head of hair forever. After he was born, one of the doctors told Judy that Steven and she had been at high risk of not making it. We had our miracle baby.

We decided to commemorate Steven's birth with a special purchase.

Since I had a lot more disposable income, thanks to the large pay increase I received for becoming the interim superintendent, we bought Steven a car that we planned to give him when he was old enough to drive. We didn't just buy a car either, we bought a dream car: an S300 Mercedes.

We put a "Steven" license plate on that car and parked it in the garage. That purchase felt like the perfect way to celebrate a special event.

No matter how busy I got while in Rockford, I remained active in NABSE. We were fortunate at the time that Dr. Ted Kimbrough, the superintendent of Chicago schools, was to be the national president of NABSE, which prompted NABSE to hold its national conference in Chicago. Seizing the opportunity, I arranged for a hundred staff members to go to Chicago to take advantage of all the professional development available at the conference. Personifying how heavy-handed Bowen was, when I returned from that conference, he tried to reprimand me for using district funds. That didn't work out for him since I had a paper that had his signature of approval.

NABSE appreciated that I had made sure a larger portion of the 100 staff received financial support to attend the convention. I felt as though my effort instilled a feeling in the membership that I was a guy who could get things done.

# CHAPTER THIRTEEN

Throughout my stay in Rockford, the city remained in an uproar.
The changes brought about a lot of fighting. I saw that there was
going to be some sort of upper-level fight for the job of
superintendent. Even though I kept telling everybody I wasn't
interested in becoming superintendent, I don't think they quite
believed me. They thought I would try and make some kind of end
run to do so.

I told Judy I wanted to get out of Dodge. Dealing with the
eventual outcome wasn't going to be pleasant.

Bill Bowen's legislative support continued to try and get him
qualified to be the superintendent. But his lack of credentials
necessary to be a superintendent remained an albatross around his
neck. Getting a waiver from the state department proved to be an
uphill battle for him, but he thought through his connections he'd be
able to make that happen. Even if he didn't get the job, I could tell
that he wanted to start over. He didn't want to move forward with
any of the people that Dr. Sullivan had hired.

I surged on, staying alert to potential opportunities.

Because I was interim superintendent, and I was vocal at the
Illinois superintendent's meetings and at NABSE meetings, I met
the former superintendent of Dallas Unified, Dr. Marvin Edwards.

He'd become a superintendent in one of the Chicago suburbs. We got to be friends and we'd go to lunch together. While attending a NABSE meeting, he told me, "Bernard, you have what it takes to be a superintendent"—a full-time superintendent.

Dr. Edwards was well-known and widely respected, which made his words even more meaningful. He proved to be a wizard for fueling my confidence about being qualified to be a superintendent.

He continued. "I'm telling you, you can do it."

Then he told me they were going to have an opening for NABSE's chair of the superintendent's commission and that I should take it. Even though I was an interim superintendent, I still held the title of superintendent in the eyes of NABSE and everyone else, because officially, I was the first Black superintendent of Rockford, an official position appointed by the district's board.

Sure enough, after a vacancy came about on the superintendent's commission, I got nominated to fill the position. That's how I first arrived to the NABSE Board, leading the way for me to eventually become the chair of the superintendent's commission.

Holding that position, I told myself that it might be wise to begin applying for some of the job openings I saw in other areas of the country.

I began to apply to jobs in different locations, like the one in Washington state. The idea of heading west appealed to me. Around that same time, Judy's sister Karen suggested that I apply for the open job in West Point, Mississippi.

Judy told me, "They're so racist, you'll never get that job."

I asked her, "What's the harm in applying? As much as we go down there to visit your mother and everybody, we'll probably get a free trip out of it. They can at least fly us down there."

Judy agreed.

I applied and the situation appeared to be playing out like we figured it would. There were two Black board members, and each of them spoke to me. The gist of what they said was, "You're not going to get that job. As much as we're trying to talk you up, they just won't approve it."

They had not taken into account the Black community and all of Judy's relatives getting involved, which they did. Her family made us feel like we had a thousand relatives in West Point. The following dialogue grew familiar in the area: "We are going to demand that the best person qualified gets the job. And we know Bernard Hamilton is that guy."

I had a doctorate, and the next candidate wasn't even close to having my background. One thing led to another and they hired me.

Despite Judy's memories about growing up in West Point, returning to the area wasn't a hard sell. Once we began the interview process, she was shocked that West Point had evolved to become a different place.

The board members were very nice. After they flew me in on a private plane for one of the interviews, Judy told me, "Man, they're treating you like royalty." When I advanced further in the process, they had me bring along Judy. During that visit, they took us to an affluent area of town that Judy had never seen.

She saw where the upper-class Whites lived, an area that included a golf course that's one of the top-100 golf courses in the United States—the Waverly Golf Course—and they put us up there. Of course, they wined and dined us. The food was fabulous like nobody's business. Judy couldn't believe the high living.

We learned that the Bryans were an elite group, not only as the town's major employer, but on the school board as well as city and state governance. Bryan Foods provided West Point's main industry. The company had factories in West Point and also in Tennessee. They were movers and shakers and the entire Bryan family was actually quite liberal. They also held a high opinion about Judy. She forgot that she had been friends with one of the Bryan girls (a Harrell) and actually had gotten rides to college from one of the Bryans' daughters, who later died in an accident.

John Bryan, who had run Sara Lee for years, was the elder brother of the family. Among his friends were Bill and Hillary Clinton, and also Vernon Jordan, the former director of the Urban League on Clinton's staff. Jordan flew to West Point regularly because of his friendship with John Bryan.

Bryan's sister, Caroline Harrell, was the vice president of the school board. And one of the lawyers we met with every week in Rockford was the lawyer for John Bryan and the Sara Lee organization based in Chicago.

When I got offered the job to become West Point's superintendent, I didn't hesitate to accept.

Along with the job, they gave me an honorary membership to the Waverly Golf Course. That was pretty high living right there. Judy loved that part.

Back in Rockford, I think people realized my leaving was a foregone conclusion, particularly given all the negativity in the newspapers and on the radio. Rockford had a history of people coming and going, and they still do, so my move didn't surprise anybody once it became official.

When a lot of other folks left Rockford, the people in the area talked about the departed like they were dogs. They weren't appreciated by the community, because people in the community didn't believe they had acted properly. Conversely, I felt like the overall community sentiment toward me kind of said, "You've done well here, and you're one of the very, very few people who are leaving here with great integrity and a good reputation."

I think they appreciated the fact that I had respected their culture. I never had tried to take advantage of folks. I always talked to everybody and they liked that.

All told, we spent three years in Rockford.

# CHAPTER FOURTEEN

Heading into the position at West Point, I understood the inherent challenges that stood in front of me.

The district didn't have much money. During the interview process, they told me, "We can't pay you too much because we only have about $20,000 left in our reserve."

My reply: "You're in trouble."

In addition, the district had not made the academic gains expected by the state's standards. Because of that deficiency, they were operating under an academic warning that had advanced to the point where they were about to get placed on probation. They actually thought they were doing well. I told them otherwise, noting the fact they had never met state standards.

While negotiating my deal before agreeing to accept the position, I understood that I was making more in my job in Rockford than they wanted to pay me in West Point. I told them I wasn't expecting them to give me a raise in pay to take the job, but I did want them to match what I was making in Rockford. I'd gotten some pretty good negotiating guidance from the people at NABSE. They advised me to make sure I got my benefits initially and I'd be okay. I could worry about more compensation later.

I ended up getting a nice deal that included a good insurance package, a leased car, and expenses for professional development. I told them, "If I get you out of the red and into the black, I would expect to get raises." We worked out kind of a merit-pay thing.

My duties included being responsible for eight schools—covering kindergarten through 12th grade, more than 3,900 students, 262 teachers, and doing so on a school budget of $12 million, which I had to monitor.

My first day on the job in West Point was July 1, 1994. I began by attending a state superintendent's meeting in Biloxi. Then I began the process of meeting with school board members, teachers, parents, city leaders, and principals. Some of those meetings I scheduled for as early as 7 a.m. over breakfast. By the end of the second day, I'd met with all of the board members.

On the third day, I called an "everyone" meeting, inviting over 450 school employees to meet. My goal was to establish a line of communication as well as to gather input from everyone—parents, students, and educators. After two weeks, I had a pretty good idea about what needed to be done.

My hiring was heralded in one of the local papers with an editorial that had the headline "Bernard Hamilton: Our newest hope." The piece concluded with: "West Point schools are at a crossroads that will quickly lead to the year 2000. We think our school board trustees have picked the right man to guide our children to that horizon."

I felt like all of my experience made me more than qualified to tackle the job ahead of me. I could identify a lot of low-hanging fruit that could help improve the situation immediately. For example, they needed more money and didn't know how to raise more money. I could see from a mile away what needed to be done, starting with getting a bond passed.

I figured a $3 million bond would be needed to make the necessary improvements. Getting a bond of that amount passed might have appeared like a tough road to pave for such a poor area, but I came up with a plan that pushed the people to get behind it.

They wanted to fix up the schools. In the back of a lot of people's minds—particularly the Whites—they wanted to renovate Central High School, which had been forced to shut down because of asbestos problems and other problems. Central had been a high school prior to integration, and many of the Whites in the area had attended that high school. They were nostalgic about the place.

After taking a tour of Central, I thought that restoring the place would be a great project.

I also suggested that Central could be made into a magnet school. The Whites loved that idea as well as the idea of saving their old high school.

I reached out to Nathan Hale, the president of the National Magnet Schools Organization. Hale had written books about magnet schools, and when I had been in Rockford, we had used him to help design programs for our science magnet.

Hale came to West Point and offered his ideas about what we could do at the school. Our board president, along with one other member of the board, did not support the magnet program. The mayor seemed to lack enthusiasm as well. They all felt as though the extra money from the bond would not support a magnet school. I felt like the younger Whites were attracted to the magnet school idea. A lottery system would have limited the persons attending, which meant Whites would have been pulled from private schools. Personally, I felt like they were all too worried about how a magnet school would impact the area's private schools.

Once the dialogue began and everybody got excited about the improvements—particularly the Central renovation—everybody got behind passing the bond. The Blacks were hesitant, particularly about the Central renovation. They questioned me accordingly: "Why are you going to fix up that White school!" I assured them passing the bond would provide funding that would help all the kids. I stressed, "This is a good thing. You should vote for it."

We managed to accomplish a lot during my first year, and all under the suspicious watch of the Whites and Blacks, who composed a divided community. The composition of the area was 50-50 White and Black, about 90 percent of the kids in the school district were Black.

The Whites wondered if I would show bias toward Black children and their parents. The Blacks were afraid I would cater to the White families to ease community fear of "White flight"—White children leaving the public schools for the district's private school.

My only agenda was to do what was right. I'd always felt that if I did that, things would work out. When I first got to West Point, I told everyone, "I'm going to show you a mirror and if you look hard enough at yourself, you'll always take the high road." I showed them the mirror, they looked, and we made some things happen as a result.

Some highlights from my first year included:

- Initiating a communications process for staff, students, and parents in which their input was included in all phases of the school district's operations.

- Secured funding to acquire ten new school buses—the first new vehicles in decades.

- Implementing three new Advanced Placement courses at high school.

- Improving student test scores—an accomplishment I'm proud to say occurred at every school district in which I had served.

That $3 million bond got passed midway through my second year as the West Point superintendent. While the magnet school didn't come to fruition, Central got renovated along with two other schools. I also managed to secure funding for Tech Prep for secondary schools. Tech Prep is a program designed to help students gain academic knowledge and technical skills. Students can sometimes earn college credit for their secondary coursework.

Praise came my way for helping to get all that funding. But that accomplishment probably paled in comparison to the system-wide strategic plan I initiated that included all of the city employees, the mayor, the city council, and even the private school. I included everybody in the strategic plan. I had familiarity with such a plan getting put into place. When I'd been a principal in Las Vegas, I'd been minimally involved when a similar plan had been instituted.

To help with the plan, I reached out William (Bill) Cook, the founder of The Cambrian Group, the premier Strategic Planning

Company, who had helped bring similar plans to Las Vegas and some other big cities. The man happened to live in Montgomery, Alabama, so all he had to do was drive over to West Point. He was happy to consult on our ambitious project, and he gave us a reduced rate for his consultation. I didn't know the fellow personally, but he was pleased to know I'd been in Las Vegas when that plan had come to fruition.

Everybody, including the West Point mayor, gave me all kinds of accolades for opening up the school district to scrutiny and input. They weren't used to that. Not many areas were. Strategic planning was a new thing back then. I later found out that the city had undergone such a plan in the past. Everybody had felt as though the city had benefited from having done so, which helped bring the overwhelmingly positive view about having a strategic plan done for the school district, too.

The plan represented the input from over 300 volunteers, including teachers and administrators, parents, businessmen, and community activists. In adopting the plan, West Point became one of the first of several school districts across the state of Mississippi to enter into a strategic planning process.

The plan was designed to take participants to the core of what they believed the school district should—and could—be. The process emphasized new ideas and approaches in education during a time of rapid change and required the involvement of the total community—parents, business leaders, and school staffs. The process encompassed the entire community.

The mission statement of the plan read as follows:

The mission of the West Point School District, a diverse community united by a shared vision for its children, is to empower each student to achieve his or her highest potential through an educational system characterized by innovation, individualized instruction, and shared responsibility in a safe and supportive environment.

We had some great ideas that came out, and I was pleased with the whole process. The approval of the strategic plan represented a milestone for West Point Schools. After its passing, we began our work to immediately secure funding and apply a time line to the implementation of the plan.

Getting the bond passed, and the strategic planning, were things that really helped the school system.

I continued to visit the different schools daily and tried to work closely with the school board. We benefited from forming education partnerships with Mississippi State University, businesses, and other organizations. The academic achievement I saw pleased me to no end. I've always believed that if you work to strengthen academic achievement at the elementary school level, achievement at the secondary level will follow.

We also began an effort to strengthen arts in the school district. Highlights from those efforts included the Disciplined Based Arts in Education (DBAE) program, which provided training for teachers and brought visual art, music, and drama specialists into certain schools to work with students; and the Young People's Artist Series, which was a program that brought national artists into the schools.

Those efforts to infuse arts into the West Point School District's curriculum earned me an invitation to attend an Arts Education Focus Group offered by the President's Committee on the Arts and Humanities and the Goals 2000 Arts Education Partnership. That took place in Washington, D.C., at the Department of Education. What a grand occasion. Being involved in that brought me a big honor. West Point could take pride in the recognition of my inclusion as well.

We did love our house in Rockford, but when we went to Mississippi, I decided we weren't going to buy in the upper-class, White neighborhood. For starters, I wasn't sure we'd be totally safe there since we would have been the only Black family in the neighborhood. Besides, the houses near the golf course were too expensive for what I was making, particularly when we weren't sure about our future.

We ended up losing money on our beautiful Rockford home. Property values continued to plummet in Rockford due to the schools' problems along with the fact the taxes continued to rise. We lost money when we sold. Both of us were surprised about that, but that's one of the hazards of moving.

We ended up buying a roomy house in West Point that sat at a cul-de-sac on about two acres. We even bought a little tractor. The house wasn't all that pretty, particularly after the house we'd left. But we were happy.

Because Rockford had been so stressful and time consuming, being in West Point felt like a vacation. I couldn't believe I could go home at 5 o'clock in the afternoon—a totally, and appreciated, new experience.

Suddenly, I had more family time. The kids were still little, and it was nice to be at home with them more often. We went on more quality family vacations, like going to Disney World in Orlando and staying at the Disney Hotel.

Though still young, each of our kids had begun to sprout their own little personality.

Julie, our oldest, was in middle school and she was really getting happy. I don't know if the fact I was the superintendent had anything to do with that. She might have felt like my position afforded her preferential treatment at school; I really don't know.

Julie's intelligence was apparent. She made all As in school. Even though the West Point schools remained somewhat segregated, she had a lot of White friends.

Jasmine attended Southside Elementary. That girl loved sports from the very beginning. She had a tomboy persona and hated dresses. Even at two years old she didn't want to wear a dress. Basketball became her love, and she embraced the game. In the third grade, she won a free-throw shooting contest.

I helped start a Boys and Girls Club in West Point. The director hailed from Indiana and really loved basketball. Jasmine benefited from that. He gave her special attention and that really helped her skills develop.

Steven was a little baby and was coddled accordingly. I happened to mention the situation to Willie Larry, my barber and the school district mailman. I told him, "I just can't seem to get that boy away from his mother. She just babies him too much." My barber told me, "You've got to be careful, because women will do that. And if you don't change that, he'll always be a momma's boy." Sure enough, he was. And I feel guilty about that still.

You could say our kids had quite a different experience in West Point schools than their mother had.

Judy had never gotten over the discrimination against her when she was a kid. But she was delighted I'd gotten hired, and that the board members had been so nice to us. She was treated like a queen in her return to where she'd grown up.

West Point had definitely made progress where race relations were concerned, though the place still had a long way to go.

Nobody socialized with us much. I did visit the White churches. I had a habit of visiting the churches near the schools where I worked. I figured that's how you got to know the community and where you gained community support. We were treated well at those churches.

Nobody liked when I brought up Judy's past, and how she'd been treated as a child in West Point. The mayor complained to folks about Judy's story, and he mentioned it to me once, telling me it wasn't true what I had described in a newspaper article. I was quoted as saying, "When my wife went to school, the Freedom Fighters had to accompany her." That's what her grandfather told me. In response to that article, the West Point mayor told me, "We had a very peaceful integration."

Well, it may have been peaceful, but leading up to it wasn't so peaceful, because the KKK had circled Judy's family's house. On top of that, nobody would talk to her, so it had been a very quiet, aggressive anti situation. On the surface, you could go to those schools, but you had to suffer like she did.

They didn't like me talking about that. The editor of the paper told me he was going to write a story about Judy and me coming to West Point on the 30-year civil rights anniversary, how she had integrated the school, and how I was the first Black superintendent in the area. But he added, "I probably won't survive the story." Sure enough, they fired his butt.

Judy graciously accepted the niceness extended to us. She also rejoined the work force, as a school counselor. First, we had to endure a little controversy, though. That controversy had nothing to do with race.

The board didn't want the superintendent's wife to be working at a school in his district. Initially, that pissed us off. To the board's credit, they just didn't think that was really a good idea. We got over that, and Judy got hired as a counselor at a school in a neighboring city, Columbus.

My progressiveness helped me become highly regarded throughout Mississippi. What I was accomplishing in West Point received many accolades. I actually got asked to train other superintendents at the state level. Some actually thought I was in line to become the state superintendent—which I did not.

As for all the Mississippi stereotypes, the state proved to be more progressive than what is depicted. Yeah, there were still rednecks and a lot of historical baggage, but I was very impressed with a lot of things in the state, like Mississippi State University. I served on one of their boards and they wanted me to teach. Unfortunately, I'd already spread myself too thin. I just didn't have quite enough time to be superintendent and to do that.

A lot of people in West Point were looking out for my best interest, particularly Mrs. Harrell. If I articulated something to her that made sense for the school district, she pretty much supported whatever it was. That didn't mean there weren't some heated sessions in the board meetings. But, like any good board, they did what was best. I've been friends with all of them ever since.

Permission to travel to NABSE meetings had been a part of my negotiated contract with West Point. That allowed me to continue to grow in the organization that meant so much to me. During one such NABSE conference I attended, I ran into Dr. Ronald Epps and had an interesting conversation.

Dr. Epps had been the superintendent of educational services for Topeka, Kansas, Public Schools when they hired him to become superintendent of Rockford Illinois Public Schools in 1994, shortly before I left Rockford. Thus, he had inherited Bill Bowen's hire, the man I had such a bad intuition about. Dr. Epps told me, "Oh my gosh, that guy was terrible. I wish we would have kept you."

Of course, my leaving Rockford had nothing to do with that man.

I got a call from Charlie Mae Knight, who served as the national NABSE president from 1995 to 1997. Charlie knew me from my Las Vegas days when I founded B-CON. I referred to her as "The Living Legend," because she'd been a superintendent in California for many years, then she served on the city council. Today she serves on the school board in Palo Alto, California. Dr. Knight asked me to take a non-voting position as NABSE's chair of the national membership campaign.

I accepted her offer.

As membership chair, I was tasked with organizing campaigns and strategies to increase NABSE memberships. I had demonstrated my abilities on this front by being active in Las Vegas, and I'd been a founder of new affiliates in Rockford and the state affiliate for Mississippi.

We had approximately 140 state, regional, and city affiliates on the United States mainland, as well as affiliates in Canada, South Africa, the Bahamas, and some other international places. My charge would be to talk up memberships and to assist school staffs with new affiliates across the United States and the world.

I also supported the individual presidents with membership expansion, as well as providing them ideas to help support scholarships and ways to provide mentor support to all role groups in each affiliate, such as teachers, principals, superintendents, school board members, college professors, university presidents and their staff, parents, and students.

Each affiliate had its own priorities, so my support included drawing on members within NABSE who could be part of my committee efforts. I would push all of them to add to our national membership base when they asked for support. Many had local membership dues but did not require their members to join NABSE nationally.

There had been a lot of funny faces when I began as the membership chairman. Those in the know about my appointment said, "We appointed him the membership chairman for all of NABSE, and he's going to help increase our affiliate members." Which I did by flying all over the country and trying to get people to join. For example, I managed to get a NABSE affiliate started in Albuquerque, New Mexico, a place which never had an affiliate.

In addition to that role as membership chairman, I continued to work in my role as the chairperson of the superintendent's commission. I felt as though my career and goals were headed in the right direction. Influencing education at a national level continued to be one of my goals. NABSE gave me that opportunity.

Because I'd gained a higher national profile, I began to get heavily involved in NABSE's politics, and what a time to get involved.

Dr. Knight was dealing with a political mess while trying to make sure that NABSE's finances were solid. The organization had plenty of money, but she found out that the board members were spending money profusely without providing receipts. She also discovered that Dr. Charles Moody, who, at the time, was credited as the organization's founder, was spending more money than anyone else and the executive director alleged that he refused to provide receipts.

Dr. Knight hired Quentin Lawson to be NABSE's executive director, and he dug into the books. Lawson uncovered that Moody had $10,000 in his budget earmarked to spend however he wanted. At every convention or conference, he would have guest suites for his speakers or people he felt should be honored—whatever relationship he had with them. In addition to spending that money, he'd been taking a lot of flights to South Africa (which had a NABSE affiliate) and other places. Moody was a permanent fixture on the board and his wife served as NABSE's historian. Because of their stature, all, or most, of their expenses were being paid. That became a big issue.

After reviewing Lawson's findings, Dr. Knight put an end to Moody's spending.

When I went to a conference in San Diego, I arrived at the board meeting late, just when Dr. Moody and his wife were walking out of the meeting. Mrs. Moody was cussing about the board being no good, and that I was part of that "no good board."

Thus, one of the biggest issues going on was dealing with discord on the board.

As time went on, the board began to split between those who supported the founder and those who didn't. Dr. Lois Harrison Jones, the former superintendent of Dallas, the Unified District, followed Dr. Knight as NABSE president. She continued with the policy that expenditures required receipts. You couldn't just do whatever you wanted. Dr. Andre Hornsby became the president after Dr. Harrison and he directed the executive director, Quentin Lawson, to continue the policies of receipts for all expenditures. Dr. Moody's participation in board activities were nearly nonexistent during Dr. Hornsby's term of office.

Following Dr. Hornsby was Dr. Deloris Saunders, who had a very positive relationship with the Moody family. Dr. Saunders even appointed Dr. Moody's son as her corporate representative on the NABSE Board. Dr. Moody and his son would later sue the NABSE Board members and the organization for neglect of duty and failure to remove the executive director for neglect of duties.

Dr. Emma Epps, former superintendent of the Ecorse Public Schools in Michigan, became president after Dr. Saunders. Dr. Epps led the board to a settlement with the Moody Lawsuit, with the board later being exonerated of all charges alleged by the lawsuit. Dr. Epps also appointed a committee led by Dr. William Ellerbee, chair of the NABSE Foundation at the time and associate superintendent for the state department of education in California. The committee was charged with interviewing past members during the early years of NABSE and to research who were the founders.

Later, the facts were reviewed, and that revealed that Dr. Moody wasn't *the* founder of NABSE. A vote of the NABSE Delegate Assembly was made that Dr. Moody wasn't the official founder of NABSE, he had just been the convener of superintendents who actually founded NABSE. That declaration brought discord about who got credit for founding the organization.

# CHAPTER FIFTEEN

If you talk to any superintendent, they know they're eventually going to get fired. You're not going to have the job for life. The job just isn't meant to be long term. When I served as the West Point superintendent, the average stay for any superintendent to remain on the job was two and a half years. I don't know whether the average is the same today or not. If you remained on the job for five years, you were doing great. Every superintendent shared the belief, "You know you're going to get fired, so always do the right thing."

I remained progressive, but probably too progressive for West Point, Mississippi. Some of my hiring decisions weren't popular. If I thought the person was the best qualified, I hired them. That probably ruffled the board's feathers some. And the board didn't believe they had enough control over some of the changes I had implemented. They didn't like some of the other things I did either. I don't believe they felt as though I respected them enough.

For instance, they weren't so hot about me diversifying the AP classes. I felt their reluctance to do so stemmed from them not wanting to further integrate the classes. I won't say that was the main issue. I think my aggressiveness in pushing the district to be more progressive was more of a concern. The constant vibe I had received since my first day on the job had remained the same: "He's going too fast."

I think the board's vice president, who was from the Bryan family, liked how I went about my business. I think other board members did not share that opinion. I could sense it. And there was talk. I hadn't been hiring some of the board members' favorite people. One board member never seemed to be satisfied, and constantly looked for things to complain about. We spent a lot of time dealing with some of his negatives.

My initial contract in West Point had been for three years. Typically, by the end of the second year, if they liked what you were doing, they would increase the contract another two or three years. They increased my contract by two years. By the end of the third year I began to think, "I've got two years left, I wonder what they feel about me?"

I told my family, "If I don't get an extension by the middle of my fourth year, I'm leaving."

I expressed my concerns to the board's attorney and the board's president, and they kind of ignored what I told them. I didn't bring it up again.

Ironically, one of the things we worked on at NABSE during that juncture was the job security issue for superintendents.

Being the chairperson of the superintendent's commission, I understood that most were interested in how to support the

216

superintendents in their districts and how to try and get NABSE to get national legislation to support them—or to get the other larger, national organizations to support them.

NABSE was mostly networking among its members at that time, and supporting each other. Specifically, once a superintendent got fired—remember, this usually happened after two and a half years on average—he or she should have other NABSE superintendents to support them. While we were doing some networking, we needed to do a better job of doing so, prompting the question of how could we do better supporting each other.

Thanks to Quentin Lawson's direction, we began to compile a directory of every Black superintendent in the country. That directory gave us a master list and became a great resource that we used to help support all of the Black superintendents. Even if they weren't a NABSE member, we offered them support. We'd invite all of them to our events, and hoped that they would become members.

Because I felt as though I was one of those superintendents who needed to move on, I began applying for other jobs.

First, I applied for jobs in Mississippi. The folks in West Point began to realize I might really leave once I became a finalist for the superintendent position in Jackson. A front-page story in a

December 15, 1996, story by the *Clarion-Ledger* (Jackson) was headlined "Candidate for JPS chief gets high marks at home."

In the story, Roger Hill, West Point School Board President, noted that my leaving would put West Point in a "terrible position." He added: "He's young and aggressive and can generate a lot of ideas. … He is now getting his feet on the ground where he can run with it."

West Point Mayor Kenny Dill was also quoted in the story when he said this about me: "He's been good and involved. He's got a good personality and meets people well. He's worked hard." He added: "When somebody does a good job, you don't care to make a change."

The West Point community didn't want to lose me, particularly to Jackson. When I elected to withdraw my name from consideration for the Jackson job, the *Daily Times Leader* (West Point) heralded my decision with a story titled "Hamilton: No longer considering leaving."

Hill noted that I'd been up front with the board from the beginning of the process, as he said, "He told us right up front, and he has been straightforward with us all the time. You can't help but appreciate that. And, the fact that they were considering him for the Jackson position just reaffirms our decision to hire him. You'd worry if nobody ever came knocking on your door, asking about somebody you had hired."

I had also considered a job in Natchez, Mississippi. The problem with that one was the fact that Judy's ex-boyfriend—someone she had considered marrying—was a big shot in Natchez. One of his family relatives was a legislator, so I didn't have a good feeling about that one from the beginning. In addition, they didn't wine and dine Judy and me like West Point had when they wanted to hire me.

I told Judy that if Natchez made me an offer, we weren't going to take it. That conversation took place right before we headed to a NABSE national conference. Before we left, the Natchez people called to offer me the job. And I turned it down.

Once we arrived at the hotel where the convention was being held, I got a call from one of the legislators, who asked me to reconsider the Natchez offer. He said, "We really need you in Natchez. We'll make it right whatever it is." I told them they had a great city, but my wife's ex-boyfriend lives there, and that's not a good thing. I didn't want to insult them and tell them I wasn't crazy about the city or the way they had treated us during our visit.

David's example from the Bible has always helped serve me as a guiding principle. Like David, I've always felt as though God had a plan for me, just like he does for everyone. I always wanted to do what I thought God was leading me to. Usually, that guiding principle has made things easier for me. Just like the decision to go to West Point had been. They just opened their doors to us after we had the impression it would never happen.

If I ever did a quick, two-minute summary of all my jobs, they had all been like that. At every stop, I felt wanted. My jobs in Las Vegas, in Rockford, and in West Point all just felt like the right moves at the time. And they were.

That would be the vibe after I applied for a job in Kentucky.

They flew me in on a private plane to Owens County, Kentucky, where I addressed the school board, informing them about the accomplishments we'd made under my watch at West Point. Prior to taking the trip, Mr. Barry, one of the principals I appointed to the West Point Junior High, suggested that I touch base with Ms. Katherine Wallace, the founder of the Kentucky Alliance of Black School Educators. Mr. Barry had been involved in the Memphis Alliance of Black School Educators and was friends with Ms. Wallace.

Ms. Wallace introduced me to Mr. Gene Wilhoit, the deputy commissioner of the Kentucky State Department of Education. He had served as the Superintendent of State Department of Education for Arkansas, appointed by Governor Bill Clinton.

When he shook my hand, before he could ask how I was doing, he said, "We could use a person like you, I wish you would consider coming to work for us."

What I didn't know was, at the time, the state of Kentucky was really in a tizzy to increase the number of Black superintendents—they did not have one. The lack of Black superintendents was a big issue, and since I was a superintendent, they thought I could help them.

Wilhoit offered me the job of associate commissioner for the Kentucky Department of Education. Once again, I felt like David receiving God's plan. I accepted the offer and we moved to Louisville, Kentucky, in 1999.

Unfortunately, right about the time we moved, Julie was preparing to be a cheerleader in West Point, and she was pretty sure she'd make it. She figured that being a cheerleader in middle school would have paved the way for her to be a high school cheerleader. My move killed her cheerleading dreams. My first daughter was devastated. She had seen her dream right at the tips of her fingers, a whisper away from coming to fruition, and then her dad moved the family. To this day, I think she still has lingering bad feelings about that move.

Leaving West Point, I reflected back to Las Vegas during the period from when I'd wanted to be an intern assistant principal to when I became a principal. I remembered sitting in small groups among the many great teachers and educators in the area, and I listened, gathering information about everything pertaining to education. And I'd think, "Why can't we do this at all the schools? Why can't more kids get help? Good Lord, all this great instruction that's happening in these various schools, it should be everywhere. Why can't the superintendent make sure that happens?"

Then, while attending NABSE meetings, the thought hit me that I should go to work at the State Department for the Secretary of Education. Working in Washington, D.C., became a goal and I began thinking in terms of making positive strides nationally that would help the kids. I'd seen what could be done while at Walter Bracken; why not apply that at a national, or larger, scale?

# CHAPTER SIXTEEN

Because I went to segregated schools for much of my education, White teachers were never a part of the equation that determined my feelings about anything. I came to believe that not having to deal with White teachers helped keep intact what self-esteem I had. Since then, I've talked to a lot of folks all over the country, and I've noticed the ones who went to segregated schools—or experienced segregation in various places—are pretty strong folks.

Judy has had a pretty tough time with self-esteem. Remember what she experienced going to integrated schools? They flat out rejected her. Her stories will break anybody's heart. Like having to sit on the steps while all the other kids played because nobody was allowed to play with her. She experienced that brand of isolation all the way until she began high school, where, unfortunately, it continued. She had developed into the best rifle girl in the school when it came to flipping the gun around, but she wasn't allowed to be a rifle girl. They tolerated her playing an instrument in the band, yet that privileged position of twirling the rifle remained taboo.

The thrust of the Black middle class's efforts to help all Black kids was all about Black kids needing to go to White schools—which meant getting bused. If they didn't follow that initiative, they never would have had enough modern books or quality facilities. Integration could have worked to some extent, but two things happened. First, the Black teachers were not hired by the White schools. That meant the Black kids lost their role models. Second, while the schools were integrated, kids continued to be segregated within the schools. While a few of the Black kids got the privilege, the majority suffered. That's the case, even today.

When the subject about the notion of a Black gap is brought up, you'll hear a few White and Black civil rights school folks protesting, but their protests are never sustained. And it's not substantive enough to promote meaningful change for the majority of the low-income kids, Black and White. Blacks suffered more because they couldn't hide their color.

Middle-class kids will make it, because the system will make exceptions for a few talented middle-class kids. Still, you have the majority of the Black kids not achieving well because of this whole notion that there's not enough pie for everybody. Those who have the pie are afraid of losing their share of the pie, which is ridiculous since we know such a fear is unfounded in America, because there's plenty of pie.

I believe that an equity in resources would have helped to balance the Black-and-White equation. The tax structure should be changed to where low-income kids have equality of books and where the teachers have access to professional development and colleges so they can attain the same level of education and the students have access to the curriculum.

Black schools did not have AP, Algebra I, and chemistry classes. They didn't have the equipment for chemistry. They didn't provide enough funding so the schools had enough teachers to teach more than just basic math. Black schools simply weren't funded. Fixing that problem would have been a better solution than integration. Unfortunately, the idea of equal resources has always been a secondary solution. Folks did not fight hard enough, nor long enough, to bring that solution to fruition.

The Black middle class at the time didn't think that they could win the fight to have equality of resources. They figured they would be pushed aside with an "Oh, we don't have enough money to do that." That fight never got off the ground. And it's permeated the whole education system, even today.

Upper-middle-class Blacks never believed they could win the battle for funding. The fight for funding remains a huge battle. Black communities were left to face a dilemma. "Do we fight for the funding so we can keep our schools, and our kids have self-esteem?" Or "Do we fight for integration?"

Pick the lesser of two evils.

Integrating schools—mandatory busing did deliver a huge number of students who did achieve. Still, look at the number of the ones who have not. Even today, we're not delivering because of the inequities of society. Countless students are left to come up way short of achieving their potential.

We can second-guess and say mistakes were made, or we can say it couldn't have gone any other way. Still, that was the choice that was made, and we see the outcome.

While we lived in Mississippi, my kids had mostly White friends. Segregation still existed to some extent, but it was easier to navigate the situation in West Point than it would have been at most places. The people there were more transparent about what they were doing. All that stuff about they'll let you know, that was true. West Point people were genuinely friendly. You didn't feel any hate. We didn't encounter any more rednecks there than any of the other places we've lived. People were easy to talk with no matter where you were, the grocery store, work, school. But very few Whites would go beyond friendly relationships at work and the grocery store. What I felt at church surprised me. Nobody seemed to have a problem with the fact I served as the superintendent of the district's schools, yet the vibe we got was like, "What are you doing at our White church?"

Friendships in West Point didn't usually go past waving of the hands. We didn't receive a lot of invites to the homes of the Whites. That was different from Las Vegas. The West Coast strikes me as a little more integrated.

Everything seemed well with the family when we started out from West Point to Frankfort, Kentucky. After all, we were the Cosby Family, or so we thought.

That would change.

Once I arrived to Frankfort to begin my new position as associate commissioner for the Kentucky Department of Education, I asked Gene Wilhoit, Kentucky's education commissioner, about the expectations for the job. He told me, "One, I would like you to help us find the first Black superintendent. Two, to evaluate all of the after-school programs in the whole state." And three, he wanted me to ramp up my NABSE involvement.

During my three years in Frankfort, I did what I could to try and help find the state of Kentucky's first Black superintendent, though in one meeting, I commented—and they put my comment on the front page of the newspaper—that "If Kentucky wanted a Black superintendent, they would have had one by now."

A lot of people didn't like that statement and got pissed off about it. My point had been a valid one. I just hoped that frank observation would have gotten them pissed off enough to do something about it.

While still in Frankfort, Wilhoit encouraged me to run for the NABSE presidency and told me, "You'll get it hands down."

I'd known I wanted to run for NABSE president for some time. Because I was on the NABSE foundation board, I had a vision about where things were going in the organization. I began to see the path I could take to become president.

I realized that the first thing I needed to do was to make sure people knew who I was. Being chairperson of NABSE's membership offered visibility, and people saw my name in NABSE literature because of that position. In addition, I was on the board. But I knew I needed to gain an even higher profile if I was going to get elected president. Though I had a lot of support to become the next NABSE president, I began to campaign for the position. Hindsight would later tell me I probably spent too much of my time campaigning.

The first time I ran, I ran against Dr. Delores Saunders in April of 2003. In my mind, I just thought, "I'm a superintendent and people will vote for a superintendent." That wasn't exactly the case.

Prior to the election, NABSE had a constitutional convention, known by most as a "Con-Con." There were unusual events. During my many years in the organization, we'd only had a few. Among other things, the Con-Con's purpose was to reinstate NABSE's mission and the bylaws. While at that constitutional convention, the subject of membership was discussed by one of the committees on which I served. Unfortunately, I proposed to the committee a requirement that all members at the local levels needed to become national members. The committee voted it down. Where I got in trouble was that what I had proposed was viewed as a radical idea, even though one of our icons in the organization, Barbra Sizemore, supported it. Add to that the perception about what happened.

One of our past presidents was well respected at the time and was active in most of the committee meetings. I think it's important for people to know that the past president said, "Bernard, I'm going to get that in for you, because we should have that."

Well, I never asked for that to be done, but the past president managed to put the proposal on the agenda. The proposal got voted down. A lady on the committee, who hailed from Texas, told me, "You went against the committee. That was just wrong, Bernard."

I didn't want to throw the past president under the bus at the time, but the truth was, I did not put the proposal on the agenda, even though I had previously proposed the measure while in committee.

Later one of the Texas presidents, Ed Cline, told me, "Bernard, you lost our vote because of that."

I told Cline, who had pushed for my idea, I had not, meaning I hadn't gone against the committee's wishes. He told me, "Next time, don't listen to that person."

Texas had a bunch of affiliates, so they represented about a third of the NABSE vote. However, I still thought I could win because so many people knew me, though the past presidents at the time didn't know me that well. I was still new to them. And I was pretty independent. That fact bothered people. They were reluctant to endorse me despite how active I was in the organization. People saw me all over the place. Not gaining their endorsement bothered me a little bit. These days, NABSE presidents will offer endorsements. They remained neutral back then. Still, I'd always been a confident guy where my relationships with people were concerned. I remained optimistic about my chances of winning. The closer the election got, more members began realizing that Dr. Saunders was kind of radical, but by then my goose was cooked.

I lost by a few votes. Later, my Texas supporters including Dr. Elaine Bailey, John Washington, Dr. Melvin Gilder, and Dr. Jay Cummings (our NABSE "Demonstration Schools" genius) helped me to regain the Texas vote.

I remained on the board because I represented the superintendents. They were a very important group and they supported me and trusted me. I cared about them as much as they cared about me, so I wanted to represent them accordingly.

Dr. Saunders took office in November of 2003 and served until 2005. During her time in office, she would almost destroy the organization due to her handling of Dr. Charles Moody, who managed to split the board in terms of loyalties.

Being on the board, and being a lifetime NABSE supporter—and a believer in everything the organization stood for—I grew frustrated with some of the developments at NABSE at the time, and I wasn't the only one. The frustration level grew to the point where some board members quit attending the meetings. Still, we had to keep the organization going. I helped lead an effort to overthrow the president, or to undercut her authority.

Dr. Saunders had refused to allow the executive director, Quentin Lawson, to give us reports and to function as the executive director. As a result, we called a meeting and we decided to vote to reinstate the executive director's ability to make decisions, to meet with the conference people, and to have a budget to run the office. Because we had a good-sized staff in the national office in Washington, D.C., at that point we felt as though the executive director needed to be in charge.

Dr. Charlie Mae Knight, who had served as the NABSE president from 1995 to 1997, was a fiscal conservative. She consistently donated large sums to NABSE and bailed NABSE out of many financial crises. She was a Republican and counted Condoleezza Rice among her friends. Dr. Knight was so tight that people figured that she couldn't be anything but a Republican. She had been the one to bring in Lawson, instructing him to examine all of NABSE's finances. In the process, she insisted on the policies to go along with it. I don't think Lawson was doing anything wrong under her, because she would look at every piece of paper and every bank account herself.

Eventually, Dr. Moody and his son, C. David Moody Jr. (who was a member of the board of directors and the chairman of NABSE's audit committee), filed suit against NABSE, Lawson, and several board members in November of 2005.

The Moodys alleged that Lawson had mismanaged NABSE financially and otherwise, and that board members did not take appropriate actions to investigate Lawson's mismanagement. Further, they wanted Lawson to be removed from office.

In Dr. Saunders's effort to try and discredit the executive director—Lawson—she went to the newspapers to try and discredit him publicly rather than working to address the problem behind closed doors within her own organization. I wasn't the only one who considered Dr. Saunders's tactic to be the wrong one.

Educators live on their integrity and good name. NABSE is composed of educators. By saying that Lawson had done this and the organization had done that, Dr. Saunders had publicly put down her own organization. In response to those accusations, we began to lose memberships quickly. NABSE is a membership organization. Accordingly, NABSE depends on its members to pay dues and attend conferences. The organization needed the funds from both to operate.

Dr. Saunders said Lawson wasn't appropriating funds correctly and NABSE was going bankrupt because of him. By saying we were going bankrupt and that the organization wasn't doing well, NABSE took a nosedive, like a plummeting stock.

In addition, many affiliates across the country depended on the national organization as their support base. If the national organization became discredited, then all those affiliates suffered.

Dr. Emma Epps succeeded Dr. Saunders as NABSE president in 2005. She believed we needed to settle the lawsuit. I believed differently. The board voted to settle, and a settlement officially was reached on November 14, 2007.

NABSE had to pay upwards of $500,000, for lawyer fees and court cost. The judge felt that since NABSE had actually changed some of its practices, the organization had benefited from the lawsuit and should pay the court costs. That settlement devastated the NABSE's finances.

Lawson, who died in 2016, did many good things for NABSE. Included in his accomplishments were helping the organization find a path to get out of debt and to help get organized with new programs. However, the presidents after Saunders didn't monitor Lawson like they should have. No doubt, some of the accusations about Lawson were probably true. At the very least, he'd been too loose with the organization's money because he had too much freedom.

Dr. Deborah Hunter-Harvill followed Dr. Epps as president, serving from 2007 to 2009, which set the stage for my second bid at the presidency in 2009.

By then, I better understood the NABSE constitution that ruled. Many members had asked me to run again. I had a lot of people coming to me for direction. The corporate people were coming to me, too. I felt obligated to run because of the people who wanted me to be a part of whatever they were doing. I knew that I could perform the duties of the president because I had already been leading anyway—sometimes you don't have to have a title.

234

Primarily, I ran for president a second time so everybody would remember my name. I knew other folks had run two or three times before getting elected. I didn't want people to think that I was no longer interested in the position. The collective message I received was "Not this time, Bernard, but maybe next time."

So, I really didn't think I was going to win in my second run at the presidency. I even kind of supported the person I thought would win, Dr. Carrol Thomas, who was a superintendent out of Texas. Many thought he'd be a good president and he won the election.

In the aftermath of that election, I felt encouraged about my future in NABSE, the organization I loved. Further, I felt that future would include the presidency.

## CHAPTER SEVENTEEN

I felt as though raising a son would be different than raising daughters. A part of that feeling stemmed from the drama of my life experiences. Another part stemmed from the NABSE message that you had to save your sons.

I didn't want to be like Daddy Walt—who scared me—or my real father, "The Bear," who was not around me much. Thus, I felt like I needed a different approach with Steven than what I'd used with my daughters. I just felt like I needed to be more of a role model for him.

Steven was still a pre-kindergartner when we lived in West Point. Everybody just fawned over him. Once we moved to Kentucky, he and I began to get involved in more activities.

Though I worked in Frankfort, we lived in Louisville, 65 miles away. That created a situation that would see me drive like a crazy man on Interstate 64 to get home after work to help out with all the kids' activities.

I became one of Steven's baseball coaches at the YMCA, then I became one of his basketball coaches for two or three years. The apple didn't fall far from the tree, and he had my speed. I was surprised, and pleased, that he had that natural speed, and I found that exhilarating. Would he eventually go on to fulfil my regret of not going to the Olympics? I could see him on the podium, medal being draped around his neck, then standing tall while "The Star-Spangled Banner" played on the loudspeaker at the host city's stadium. Being fast delighted Steven to no end, too. He would outrun everybody. I couldn't wait to see him get going on the track. Once he started running track, I helped coach the team.

Judy pointed out on several occasions that I never let Steven win. She was right. My upbringing taught me that you shouldn't just let a child win automatically. You should give them something to shoot for, and one day they will beat you. I never let Steven beat me running, and he was fast. I learned later he was very sensitive and a great poetry writer.

Looking back at how our kids were when they were young amazes me. They had been model citizens. They were good students, making all As and Bs, and they never got in trouble at school. They all had perfect attendance. All three were great students.

Our kids had just about everything you could think of growing up. We wanted them to have the things we didn't have when we were kids. They probably had things too good. Throughout my early life, I had little. Judy was fortunate to not want for much from her family and she benefited from a very close-knit family structure. And all eight of them went and finished college. Judy had that whole family village when she was growing up. Judy and I didn't have that with our family since we moved around so much. And we didn't have that many friends.

While we didn't want our kids to want for too much, I constantly tried to balance the easy life with what I believed: If you have to do a bunch of chores, and if you don't get much, you're hungrier.

I always thought you should earn the money you spent. The whole idea of delayed gratification builds character. Judy didn't seem to feel that way. She came from a tight family. They played games together. They still play games when they get together now. Every Christmas they try to put a puzzle together. Her father started that tradition. The puzzles will have like a thousand to two thousand pieces. I don't know how they do it, but they figure it out.

I made sure our kids had all the sports stuff, and any things that were needed to support extracurricular activities, whether it was dance, baseball, basketball, whatever. And Judy made sure we had a Christmas tree full of stuff.

We had no warning signals about the coming storms we would face.

238

# CHAPTER EIGHTEEN

As I noted earlier, my time in Frankfort ended in 2002 after three years. I then moved over to the Jefferson County School System, which is the Louisville school system. Happily, that put an end to my daily commutes between Frankfort and Louisville.

My first assignment was to become the interim principal at Hazelwood Elementary. The powers that be promised me they would then move me into the central office.

Given my background, whipping a school into shape was old hat, and a cakewalk for me. The problems at said schools stuck out like a sore thumb, and were always the same problems.

The first thing that is noticeable is the principals at such schools did not have a lot of contact with the teachers or the kids. Such principals operate like, "Calm down, do as I say or else."

In general, one of the things most principals at said schools are guilty of is not doing their paperwork at night—after the kids are gone. During the school day, they should have their bodies in the classrooms. They need to constantly be talking to kids, parents, and teachers. Doing so raises the kids' expectation because they see that somebody cares about them—and I always had a policy of letting interested parents go into the classrooms.

If I'm standing right there in the classroom, I'm following up on the expectations I've already expressed to the teachers. They should know what I want them to do, because I've already announced what I want globally. Just being there is enough. I don't have to say anything. They just rise to the occasion.

I've already told the teachers at the staff meeting that no teacher should be sitting at their seat. If I see a teacher sitting at their seat, I'm not pleased. Teachers should be instructing and reinforcing the kids, so I told them I expected them to be walking around the classroom while they teach.

As the principal, I make sure I go into classrooms at least twice a day. Every class.

Just like with the principals, I don't want teachers to be doing their paperwork while they're at school. That's a huge problem at most schools across America. I also tell my teachers that I don't expect any of them to be doing worksheets—you're explaining to the kids what they need to know.

Teachers also need to know the curriculum so they're teaching in the right direction. I'm one of those old-time teachers and principals who know how to teach and know what you're supposed to teach. Unfortunately, most principals either don't know how to teach or aren't interested in teaching. I was always a very good clinician. I knew the curriculum and I know the instructional methods.

At NABSE, we always said—and this comes from Ron Edmunds—"we know everything we need to know to make sure that every kid learns at a high level. It's just a matter of will. If we're willing to make sure every kid learns at the highest level."

Hazelwood turned out to be one of the worst-performing schools in the state. I took on that familiar challenge, and in one year, the school's scores jumped. A lot of people were impressed by the improvement.

Interesting enough, the central office downplayed the accomplishment. After one year at Hazelwood, they came to me and asked, "Can you do it again?"

I told them I could turn around a school any time, that it wasn't a big deal. They followed up by asking if I could work my magic again. I told them I could turn any school around, no big deal.

Accordingly, they assigned me to be the interim principal at Bates Elementary, which had mostly kids from low-to-middle-income families and a few Black kids. Just like Hazelwood, they were underperforming, and just like at Hazelwood, the scores jumped under my watch.

After that year at Bates, the central office told me they had a teaching job for me. And I told them, "You don't have a very good memory. You told me point blank that you guaranteed me a position in the central office."

They created a position, Title 1 Specialist, for me. Then I spent the rest of my career there. Because of my degree and experience, the Title 1 Specialist job had a decent salary, six figures. I did that and worked with middle school principals. Even though I didn't get a title, I was helping the principals through the Title 1 office.

I retired in 2014.

# CHAPTER NINETEEN

You find out how kids turn out is about choices. Further, kids need a lot of support. They need to be exposed to adults and young people who are headed in the right directions. Choosing the wrong friends can derail that. Where our kids were concerned, we saw some friends we thought were the right friends for them, but they had their own little secrets. Judy would later reflect that our kids didn't really start having issues until they began hanging around the wrong kids in high school. Bad choices followed. Then the bottom began to fall out. I could see it happening, gradually, and I'm thinking, "If they keep going down this road, it's not going to work."

Like any parent put into that type of situation, I struggled to come up with ways to right the ship. It's humbling and frustrating to find you don't have the power to fix things the way you would like. Particularly when I had a history of fixing messes in my professional career. Some of the stuff that eventually happened involving my kids, I knew would happen. I didn't want to say it out loud, but I wasn't surprised.

Judy continued to tell me I was too strict with the kids. Our oldest, Julie, kept telling me she was going to get pregnant, which was her way of telling me I was too strict. After she did get pregnant at age 17, she was like, "See, I told you, you're too strict."

Like a lot of fathers do, I acted like mister sergeant in the Army. Funny, too, because I remembered the behavior of a father who wouldn't let me date his daughter because he was so strict. The guy had been a policeman in Las Vegas. Later I found out that girl I wanted to date had a lot of problems. From observing that girl's father, I should have learned something about how not to behave as a father. I didn't.

Steven adored Julie and so looked up to his sister. Julie was very pretty—still is. Steven was 12 when he learned about her pregnancy. That crushed him. After hearing the news, he hid behind a chair. That struck me as a cross between shame and hurt.

Judy and I were equally shocked. I just got knocked off my rocker. I felt embarrassed and upset. I had no idea about what to do. That pregnancy humbled me.

Julie had cruised through middle school. She was a self-learner, made good grades, all As and Bs. As I noted earlier, our move from West Point to Louisville had been hardest on Julie. She had earned a spot on her middle school's cheerleading squad and she had really good friends. She was the most upset when we moved. Once we moved, she again wanted to be a cheerleader, and she finally made the squad. Unfortunately, she had to quit because she was pregnant.

I did admire the way she handled her pregnancy.

She insisted on going to the regular school instead of hiding at one of the schools that helped kids in her situation. She graduated from high school and then went on to the University of Louisville.

Julie's pick of boyfriends wasn't good. The father wasn't interested in their son, Jayden, who was born in 2006. The guy probably had kids from two or three girls.

Julie lived with a guy in the dorm at Louisville and this guy turned out to be physically abusive. I would learn that he'd beaten her up many times. Still, they moved in together to an apartment that was in Julie's name. Later, an episode between Julie and that guy would prompt me to go that apartment and kick him out. During the confrontation, the kid's mother showed up and actually threatened me. By the time the police arrived, I showed them that the apartment was in Julie's name. The boy's mother left after that, taking her son with her.

Julie ended up moving into Family Scholar House, a place that helped abused girls and women get through college by providing them with funds, housing, and many other things. She actually lived on the Louisville campus at this place that was famous all by itself. Louisville has received all kinds of awards for saving young girls from abusive boyfriends.

By the time Julie finished college, she had another child with a different father. I give her a lot of credit for managing to do so. What she accomplished was amazing. She's a fighter. And we adore our grandkids.

Julie's pregnancy clearly affected Steven. Afterward, he stopped liking Black girls for whatever reason. I wondered if that was a reaction to her pregnancy.

Steven was a sweet boy, but he was immature. For example, we think he believed in Santa Claus until he was 14. When he finally discovered the truth about Santa Claus, he got mad at his mother and me. After all, we had lied to him about Santa Claus. That seemed to have really hurt him.

Steven and Jasmine had always been close, but they got closer in Louisville.

Jasmine continued to love basketball. She made the middle school basketball team in Louisville and worked hard in school. Basketball briefly became a struggle when she didn't believe she was getting enough playing time on the team, but after she earned a spot on the AAU team, her outlook changed.

Steven had been in kindergarten the last year we lived in West Point, and started the first grade in Louisville, attending the elementary school where his mother worked. Judy changed schools after that year and Steven followed her to her next elementary school. Things were going well. Throughout elementary school, Steven's mother was his counselor, and the teachers probably gave him a little extra help because of his mother.

Steven was a good-hearted boy. He enjoyed Sunday school, and he absorbed all of our preaching about Christ. I felt proud about how loving he was to everyone. He worked hard at school, too. Then at middle school, he began to experience disappointments. Judy and I would later feel that his middle school years served as a harbinger of things to come. What he experienced during those years led him to give up on himself.

Steven never wanted to be around anyone who wasn't making good grades. I felt as though he possessed an anti-loser mentality. He wouldn't tolerate kids who weren't headed in the right direction. Most of the kids getting good grades at his school were White, so most of his friends were White.

Why were the Black kids the losers?

As a lifetime educator, the only pulse I have on that was the fact that racial dynamics are a real problem in our country, like they are in many other countries. The White privilege really complicates the relationships with Black and White. When I say the White privilege, I mean White folks don't cross the line too much, and

Blacks have a sense about that. Instead of getting too close to Whites, they kind of hedge on the relationships because they don't trust them. When it comes to expectations inside the classroom, you have the problem that most teachers are female and most are White.

White females are brought up a certain way. That leads to certain ideas about behavior. If they've never had any relationships with Blacks, and their parents have shunned them from having those relationships because they're more protective of the girls, then they don't have any idea, or sense, of the Black culture. As a result of that, they're going to treat the Black kids differently. And because the boys are more dangerous to White girls in the minds of White parents, those teachers are harder on those Black boys.

Boys can't sit still to begin with. Add to that a teacher who has a fear of Black boys and you have a problem.

White middle-class parents are training their kids to sit still all along, reading to them early in their lives, so their kids have a better understanding of when they need to sit still. On the other hand, if you have a Black middle-class boy, he's more independent, more free or self-assured. Even though he knows how to sit still and read, he's not as concerned about it as the White boy. He ends up getting the same punishment as the boy who can't read, because you have got to sit still and be quiet in the classroom, or else. And that's confusing to the middle-class boys. Some of them take it the wrong way and join the lower-income, less-achieved Blacks, assuming an attitude of "You don't care about us anyway so we're just going to be up in your face."

You have some who don't have that reaction. Instead, they say, "No I'm not going to do that. I know where I'm going, and I'm going to be like my parents and I'm going to be sure that I don't get stuck in that rut."

A problem comes when some of them try to do both. They want to hang with the cool Black kids—the athletes who are liked by the girls—and they're also trying to do well in school. They find out that it doesn't work and they get sucked into being a troublemaker early on.

That's what happened with Steven.

Steven got off to a bad start in middle school.

First came the incident with his hair, which he wore in braids. The middle school principal made him take his braids down. Steven didn't understand that. His reaction was something like, "Why are you doing this? Because I'm Black?"

Like it or not, braids were against the rules.

I served as a parent representative on a council that voted to change that rule, but we lost by one vote. And the principal continued to insist on no braids, so Steven had to make the change.

Then Steven didn't make the basketball team, which devastated him. After all, Jasmine and he were best friends. They shared a love of basketball, which made the hurt of not making the team worse.

Jasmine continued to be a tomboy to a large extent. She shunned dresses from age two on up, and had been totally into sports from the beginning. Steven and she were two years apart. They became playing buddies early on. They played a lot of sports together, basketball especially. He wanted to be a basketball player like his sister and never thought otherwise. Then he wasn't.

If the hair and the basketball weren't enough, Steven struggled in math and got his first bad grades. That really brought him down. He'd never made anything but As before that.

We got him to a math tutor two or three times a week. I also suspected that he didn't have a good teacher, so I confronted the principal about the teacher, who turned out to be a social studies teacher.

After I looked over one of Steven's math assignments, I noticed that something was wrong. I complained to his teacher about that assignment and told her, "That doesn't make sense, that's wrong." All of a sudden, Steven started making Cs in math. He had a bad situation there. The next year she got fired.

Steven survived his middle school disappointments and moved on to high school where he played in the band. Everybody in the band seemed to love him and he loved being a part of the band. One day, some White friends of his wanted to goof off. Steven wanted to take part in the fun and he looked up a girl's dress when she stooped over. Not only did Steven get disciplined, he got shunned. Shortly after that, he quit the band.

Things really went south after that.

Steven didn't make the "A" track team, which shouldn't have been considered any kind of embarrassment considering the track team was the best in the state. He didn't quit though, and stayed out there for two years. He even managed to win a couple of races after he'd matured and got into shape. Steven earned a ring for his efforts and was so proud of winning that ring.

I felt really close to Steven. I drove him to band and track practice. I'd taught him how to ride a bicycle, how to drive a car, and how to drive a car with a stick shift. All the while, I tried to be a good role model.

I don't know why riding in a car affected him the way it did. No matter where we went in the car, he always fell asleep. The car just made him sleepy. So we had concerns about him falling asleep while he was driving. Of course, by the time he got to high school, drugs might have induced that sleepiness.

Another time during his high school years, we took Steven to the doctor because he couldn't sleep. Later we found out that the likely cause had been the fact he'd been taking pills. In hindsight, Judy said the doctor should have recognized that Steven had a drug problem. In any event, none of those incidents, or his behavior, managed to fully open our eyes to a problem. We just thought he either wasn't feeling great about things at school, or this or that. If we had any suspicions at all, they were minor ones, because we didn't really have any warning signals. No marijuana use, or anything like that.

By the time Jasmine was a senior, she was dating a White boy. They had been best friends through basketball and they'd been around each other since elementary school. They went together to the prom, which delivered my first major horror as a parent—more so than hearing that my daughter was pregnant.

Louisville got drenched by a rainstorm that wouldn't quit the night of the prom—thunder and lightning all over the place. At 2 o'clock in the morning, I got the telephone call every parent feared. When I answered the call, I heard: "Your daughter's been in an accident."

The accident had taken place less than half a mile from where we lived. I hurried over to where the accident happened. Fortunately, Jasmine and her date are alive.

The boy had been driving, and he was drunk as a skunk. Jasmine was drunk as a skunk, too. He'd been thrown from the car, and the car finished ominously on its side. Jasmine had been riding in the passenger seat. Because the car had flipped, she got tossed into the back seat. They couldn't get her out of the car.

Lightning continued to crack everywhere and the car rested near an electrical pole. Away from the car, they were trying to help the boy, tending to his neck and back injuries. That accident left him in bad shape, causing him to be in all kinds of braces for about a year after the accident.

The paramedics and firefighters on the scene were keeping all the spectators back because of the lightning.

I watched in horror as they tried to free Jasmine from the car. Finally, they got her loose.

I found out they had a bag of liquor in the trunk, which they had gotten from Julie's boyfriend, Jordan, who would become the father of Julie's second child.

Fortunately, Jasmine survived that night without any physical ailments.

She earned a full ride to the University of Kentucky for academics, but basketball still consumed her and she wanted to continue playing. Walking on at Kentucky would have been tough to do, so we ended up visiting Bellarmine College, a private Catholic school in Louisville. In addition to presenting Jasmine basketball opportunity, the school had a good reputation for sports medicine, physical therapy, and nursing.

Jasmine and I talked to the coach together. He told us she could try to walk on. If she made the team, she would have the opportunity to move up, which is exactly what happened. She walked on and got to play periodically the first couple of years. If you asked me to grade her basketball skills, I would say shooting was her strongest suit followed by the fact she played solid defense. Unfortunately, she had some issues with some girls on the team, and one of the coaches. They were gay. Jasmine was embarrassed and had problems with that situation. She gravitated to the other girls on the team, who were weed smokers. She might have already been smoking weed at the time, but her use escalated in college.

254

One of her best friends, who was the best player on the team, got kicked off the team for smoking weed and Jasmine had been in her room when she got caught. Jasmine's friend took the blame for all of it, which allowed Jasmine to remain on the team. But during her junior year she got into trouble for continually smoking weed. She wasn't allowed back on the team. That depressed her and drove her to increase the amount of weed she smoked. She still managed to graduate with a 3.5 average, obtaining a degree in Kinesiology. We were proud of her.

During Steven's senior year of high school, he'd been driving around with some friends when they got pulled over by a police officer. They had liquor in the back of the car. In addition to being the driver, Steven was the only Black in the car. All he got was a warning. Later, I told him, "If you weren't on the right side of town with the right color in the back seat, you wouldn't have gotten away with a warning." That was a reality we tried to explain to him. But most Black males have to live through such experiences.

We thought Steven had an alcohol problem, which we first got a hint of when he passed out during an end-of-the-year celebration after his senior year. Later we learned the circumstances of that incident.

He'd wanted to drive to a concert in Bowling Green, Kentucky, because the love of his life was going to be there. I had not allowed him to attend. In addition to the alcohol he drank, Steven also took drugs that night. At the time, we thought he'd only been using alcohol and that his behavior was simply typical high school behavior. I would later read in his journal that my decision to not let him drive to Bowling Green had bothered him to the point that he not only took pills, but he took "extra" pills.

Steven's friends loomed in the background. They were into drugs. Steven had not made good choices when picking out his friends.

Steven graduated from high school and got accepted to the University of Kentucky, making me one proud father. I supported Kentucky basketball and Louisville football. His decision to go there surprised me, but I was like, "Isn't this great? He wants to go to the flagship school of the state."

In advance of his freshman year that fall, he attended a summer bridge program in Lexington at the University of Kentucky. Later that summer, we received a call by a person in the program, who told us, "We think your son is on drugs."

All the signs were there to alert us to a problem; whether we refused to acknowledge those signs, or we just weren't equipped to handle the truth, we didn't do anything.

Steven completed his freshman year at Kentucky and returned home for the summer. That summer our home felt like a fast-food drive-through—he had many visitors to the house. Normally we'd see a car pull up, then Steven would get in the car and they'd drive off. That summer he also went to Lexington a lot to "visit friends."

Steven embraced the TV show *Breaking Bad*. He loved everything about that show. I didn't like what that show represented even though it was really popular and it stayed on the air for a long time. I just couldn't approve of how they glorified the exploits of someone operating a meth lab, I didn't care how good of an actor Brian Cranston was.

Steven would tease that he could make money by going to Mexico and selling, just like the guy on *Breaking Bad*. He even had a *Breaking Bad* poster on the wall of his bedroom.

Based on what we observed, and what he admired, we probably should have been more perceptive about what was happening in his life.

# CHAPTER TWENTY

In the midst of the turmoil Judy and I were experiencing with our kids, I made my third bid at getting elected as the NABSE president.

The year was 2012—nine years after my first attempt—and this time around, I had a pretty good idea I would win, even though I ran against three strong candidates, including George McKenna, the famous principal I mentioned earlier in the book.

A lot of people figured McKenna had the inside track based on his high profile and the success he'd had in Los Angeles—which led to a book and a movie chronicling that success.

Well, I won, bringing me a great deal of satisfaction based on what NABSE meant to me and how I had served the organization for so long. Ultimately, I believe I got elected because of my body of work within the organization, my service to the organization, and the fact I knew everybody in the organization.

Along with the satisfaction of getting elected, I felt a sense of anticipation about what I hoped to accomplish during my term as president. I had lofty goals for the organization. I hoped to beef up the state and city affiliates so they could become a big recruiter of teachers, principals, and superintendents. That was a big issue in the country, and a huge issue in Kentucky. And, of course, I had the support to do that. I also wanted to visit as many affiliates as possible to really push scholarships within the organization and to have national African American male summits all across the United States. Man, did I ever want to get out there and better the organization.

Unfortunately, what took place the night of my inauguration would prove to be a precursor for the coming years. Talk about foreshadowing.

NABSE's induction ceremony has always been a grand event. The organization makes a big deal out of the occasion to where you almost feel like royalty. This is supposed to be a happy time, sort of like the king gets crowned, the queen gets crowned. NABSE does a real production with their leadership. Feels like the Democratic Convention, only more formal, complete with tuxedos and evening gowns. There are video testimonials, speeches, and all that, too. You—the president-elect—walk in accompanied by the 20-member board. Of course, you're going to be inducted, and after you're inducted, you're going to be the president.

Nashville hosted NABSE the year of my induction. I'd arrived early, and Judy, who worked as a high school counselor at the time, was set to meet me for the ceremony scheduled for a Saturday night.

On Friday morning, Judy received a phone call while she prepared to accompany some of her high school students on a bus that would take them for a tour of the University of Kentucky. A caller from the Lexington jail was on the other end of the line. Our son had been arrested.

The episode took place in the fall of Steven's second year at Kentucky. The school discouraged living in the dorms unless you were a freshman, so he shared an apartment with two other students. They had hosted a party that got busted. Steven was the one found with the weed. There had been paraphernalia for coke, but they didn't have any coke in the apartment, just weed.

Judy called me in Nashville. During our conversation we discussed if it might be better for Steven to spend the night in jail in order to learn a lesson. We could have quickly bailed him out of jail, but Judy and I had mixed feelings. Having an idea about the path on which he'd been traveling, we wondered if getting him immediately out of trouble was the right thing to do, even though we had people telling us, "You really don't want him to stay in that place."

We'd always felt that if something like this ever happened to any of our kids, we needed to leave them in there for at least a little bit so they would learn their lesson.

Judy drove to Nashville to join me that Friday night. Neither of us could sleep. She began to waver, thinking it was a bad idea to leave him in jail. She wanted me to get him out. I told her I thought it would be a good idea for him to see what jail was like.

"But he might be raped." Judy was panicked.

I told her, "I don't think we should bail him out. Because he needs to stop this drug thing."

Sadly, on what should have been a grand occasion at my swearing in, Judy and I were preoccupied with our duties as parents. Our son had been arrested. What was the best way to handle what had happened?

Judge Angelita Blackshear Dalton, who would swear me in, sat next to me on the stage. She was a spiritual woman. I told her that all I could think about was my son. And I shared with her what had happened with him. My eyes were watery with tears. I figured everybody thought I was a big shot celebrating, and I'm thinking, "Some celebration this is." That was a bad situation. I couldn't celebrate. People might have thought I was celebrating. But I wasn't.

The judge began to talk to me how she tried to help those who came to her court. She encouraged them to find Christ. We prayed together on stage. She gave me her card and told me everything would be okay. She said to call her if we needed to advocate through the court system. Having her there was a comfort.

All of the induction ceremonies I'd seen had been grand occasions. Each president has his or her own unique celebration. During a couple of the ceremonies for women presidents, I'd seen their sororities sing and bring flowers to the stage. Maybe 100 people would come on stage. NABSE always did something fancy.

My ceremony included past presidents and some kids, who I had helped. One in particular, Chase Sanders, I helped get a job with President Obama. He opened President Obama's mail. He lived down the street from us and happened to be a friend of Steven's and Jasmine's. His father sold us our house. Chase, Dr. Charlie Mae Knight, and Dr. Sandra Ledford also spoke to my past and future leadership for NABSE. A video about me played on a large screen, and I made a speech. Again, this is supposed to be a happy time, sort of like a coronation.

Steven was all I could think about. I don't even remember the speech I made that night.

Once we returned to Louisville, we hired a lawyer who got him off, getting his charges reduced to nothing. He'd spent seven days in jail.

To this day, Judy wonders if we made the best decision on how we handled Steven's situation. I still believe we made the best decision, but that was one of the hardest weekends of my life.

While we were upset about Steven's arrest, we were also in shock at what had happened to our family. We were having problems with all three kids, and Judy's saying, "What did we do to deserve this? We don't even have liquor in our house, and we don't smoke or swear. What's happening, God? What's going on?"

Judy and I had our own personal issues like most husbands and wives, but we didn't think those would knock our kids down. She always made sure she was very close to them. Remember, she didn't even work the first five years we had kids so she could be with them all of the time. But she was in shock. I was in shock.

Judy and I continued to be stunned about our family, which continued to spiral out of control, seemingly no matter what we did.

Like with Julie, Jasmine always seemed to be with guys who would have been deemed undesirables. With Steven, we were shocked that he'd fallen so deep into drugs. When I say deep, he was deeper than we knew. But we didn't know enough about drugs to be that smart about drugs ourselves.

## CHAPTER TWENTY-ONE

When I began my duties as the NABSE president, I believed the organization would be on sound financial ground. Instead, I discovered we were in bad financial shape. That changed many things, including my grandiose plans to help improve the organization. In my first year, I realized most of my attention needed to be directed to a financial cleanup. NABSE's good name had been run into the ground. A lot of the corporate people and superintendents weren't supporting us. Thus, the cleanup job.

For starters, I found out that the office staff—that's Quentin Lawson and staff—had not done their due diligence with the taxes. Some of the finances were bad. That didn't take long for me to figure out.

Quentin had left his position as executive director before I came aboard. Earlier, after the court had cleared NABSE and its board members of any wrong (as alleged in the Moody Lawsuit), I advised Quentin to consider stepping down to help calm the waters for NABSE's future. But, he told me, "I want to prove my good name." So, at the end of Dr. Carroll Thomas's presidential term, he announced his retirement during a board meeting.

I had to respect Quentin for his decision to stay on. He and I had worked on many projects including the housing committee, the male summit, the principals' institute, the superintendents' summit, and partnerships with other educational organizations (such as AASA, ASCD, and the Council of Great City Schools). Dr. Thomas assigned me, the president-elect at the time, the task of training the newly appointed affiliate representatives to the NABSE Board, even though this was actually part of Quentin's job responsibilities. They had expanded from one affiliate representative to six. I was honored to take on one of the goals that I had made promises about during my campaign. Addressing the needs of the national and international affiliate members was an honor. We had many outstanding affiliates but the communication to them and between them had need of much work.

Dr. Betty Gray, Dr. Elaine Bailey, and Dr. Lois Johnson were recruited by me to organize the affiliates unto a united group. I asked Dr. Russell Hopewell to help lead the group as he was the affiliate representative in the Northeast.

Our affiliate presidents appreciated the communication received from NABSE through the affiliate representatives. I had worked with many of the presidents in the past, and appreciated the hard work done by those that I mention here: Dr. Betty Gray, Dr. Keith Greer, Dr. Elaine Bailey, Ms. Wanda Brooks, Mr. Dwight Bonds, Dr. Lois Johnson, Dr. Geneva Stark Price, Ms. Adrian Layne, Ms. Gloria Noland, Dr. Shirley Ison-Newsome (creator of our NABSE creed), Dr. Ed Cline, Dr. Jackie Harriot, Dr. Ken Fells, Dr. Sandra Carpenter, Dr. Katherine Wallace, Ms. Gerri Bohanan, Ms. Janice Lee, and many others. Of these presidents, Dr. Betty Gray's passion for the affiliate work was noteworthy. She organized the goals, procedures, and responsibilities in such a way that any new affiliate could easily follow her newly created manuals from NABSE.

I had not worked on any financial projects with Quentin or any NABSE presidents during my prior board member positions. Even though Quentin had been telling the board that we were running in deficits year after year, the board wasn't listening. He got blamed for that. But the boards never did do an adjustment based on the fact they were running $500,000 to $600,000 in the hole every year. A few board members asked questions about the financials, but there was never any action taken that would stop significant deficit spending.

As president, further investigation prompted me to tell the organization, "Do you realize in 2001 you got fined by the IRS for not filing your 990 on time?" The organization had gotten fined and interest had accrued that needed to be paid. In some cases, payroll taxes weren't paid. That's illegal. Officers and staff members could have been held responsible.

Everybody was shocked about all the stuff I uncovered that dated at least ten years back prior to my taking over as president.

Quentin's departure had left the organization without an executive director. Dr. Thomas, the president in place before I took over, had felt as though we should have a new executive director named by the end of his presidency. The Search Committee had serious concerns about the finalist, as well as if NABSE had the funds to pay for the new executive director. The vote for the new executive director was split down the middle. A year later we were without an executive director and still in major deficit waters. I volunteered to be executive director and president until we were in better financial health. I would only do it if the board approved my status for no more than $1 a year.

My support from the NABSE Board in hindsight was pretty solid. The officers, especially President Marietta English and Treasurer Doreen Barrett, always gave me honest feedback and were reliable once we made a board decision to move in a specific direction. Even though there were two or three board members who were a challenge, the majority of the NABSE Board were attentive to our mission and supported our efforts, especially our efforts to become financially solid again.

Another board member, Dr. LaRuth Gray, who would become a great supporter and friend during my term in office, was the president's appointed government liaison for NABSE and had contacts within the White House. She knew many White House staffers, and New York University hired her from time to time to be a lobbyist. She had a lot of vision.

I found out that Dr. Gray had quietly helped other presidents, always remaining in the background. True to form, she helped me behind the scenes with all kinds of stuff. She's as smart as all get-out. Officially she ran all of NABSE's professional development during my term as my appointed chair of professional development. Her national contacts across the country continued to provide NABSE with support from many venues. Dr. Gray had been a superintendent and was serving as a deputy director of Metro Center at New York University while serving NABSE. Her understanding of our financial crisis and guidance to the NABSE Board was a tremendous pillar of support.

Given my NABSE experiences, and what was happening with my kids, this had to be the most stressful period of my life. At one point I broke out in hives and I couldn't walk. I could barely get out of my bed to go to the bathroom during the Detroit Conference, I was so eaten up with stress.

During my term as NABSE president, I didn't do all I wanted because of some of the financial restrictions that needed to happen, but I'm satisfied with what we accomplished. I think the organization is in a much better place today.

Prior to my term, the corporate support had gone south, and I think I helped reestablish that. Corporate support was important for our partnerships as well as our financial well-being.

I instituted a corporate plan where different corporations could join the partnership at a certain level. My Corporate Partner Network, or CPN, brought former and new corporate supporters to our conferences. We established a year-long partnership beyond just one conference that included partnerships with our affiliates throughout the country.

I think I reestablished some of the confidence in NABSE with the affiliates. The communication with them was not good at the time, and I made sure they could call me at any time, or they could call the office and get help.

NABSE continued to gain strength through its commissions also. The Teachers or Instructional & Instructional Support Commission was one in point. Gerri Bohana asked if she could spearhead a Teacher Leadership Summit. I approved her proposal and she promoted the summit through our NABSE monthly newsletter, which she also spearheaded. It was a hit with our teachers, support staff and administrators.

We also instituted a "NABSE School Volunteer Day" for every city our conference visited. At those cities, we would go to two or three schools and volunteered as readers, painted their school, or partnered with companies to provide new technology such as computers and state of the art "white boards." Ron Williams, a NABSE Board member from Detroit, coordinated this effort with great success.

I reinstituted the African American Male Summit. We hadn't had that for several years, and I got that going again. And it's still going strong now. We also had not had an *NABSE Journal* for some time and this became one of my priorities. The *NABSE Journal* and the Moody Institute were vital to our membership and I appointed Dr. Lloyd Sain to continue the outstanding work that had been established by Dr. Wesley Boykin, the former editor of the *NABSE Journal* and Moody Institute. One of my longtime friends from AASA, Dr. Sharon Adams Taylor, provided me with the contacts that established a partnership to secure funding for our *NABSE Journal*. NABSE had published *Saving the African American Child* through one of its task forces in 1984. That report guided much of our work as administrators. Also, Dr. Hugh J. Scott, one of NABSE's founders, published *The Black School Superintendent: Messiah or Scapegoat?* in 1980, which also provided needed counseling to our superintendents in NABSE. Both of these publications had been highlighted in our *NABSE Journal*, which provided exemplary professional development to our membership and those interested in education for all children.

Part of the financial thing was making sure we had consistent audits. We didn't have audits that were consistent, and we hadn't been paying the IRS consistently. We owed them money from getting fined from not doing our 990s on time. I made sure that all the past 990s were done for the IRS and kept those current. To help ensure that would continue, I implemented some systems, and hired the right people, like the accountant I hired, she kept up with all the IRS stuff and did a great job. She's still there today. Both the accountant, Rhonda Richardson, and the new office assistant, Bernadette Walker, were D.C. residents and were recommended by Lois Hopson Reeder, our NABSE Board member who represented the Retired Educators Commission. Reeder also recommended a new attorney, Robert Bunn. All three have been employees with NABSE since my presidential term ended.

Finally, I helped save the NABSE building in Washington, D.C.—one of two African American buildings on Capitol Hill—which stands a block from the U.S. Senate Building. Everybody in the organization carried a sense of price about the three-story building that sat a block away from the Senate Building. We were in jeopardy of losing that building, which would have been a symbol of a real failure if we had done so. I wasn't about to let that happen while I was president.

# CHAPTER TWENTY-TWO

Steven flunked out of the University of Kentucky during his second year. We realized by then that he had waded pretty deep into the drug waters. I figured he was selling his minor stuff to get money to buy whatever he was buying. Once everything was out on the table, there were times Steven would make jokes about the situation. He'd be like, "Just be glad I'm not doing heroin." But we realized he was doing cocaine. That bothered us a lot. Cocaine addiction is serious, and a cocaine habit is expensive. We suspected that he might have been using heroin as well.

He returned to Louisville. At first, he worked odd jobs while living with friends, moving back and forth between different apartments. According to Jasmine—still Steven's best friend—the guys he was living with were heavier drug users than Steven. We were worried about him and kept telling him he could come home, but he wouldn't. We could tell he'd lived on the street some because of how filthy he was. We didn't know if he'd been there a day, two days, or three. We knew it was more than a couple of days, though. He had another brush with police during this period. This one brought more dire consequences.

A parole officer confronted Steven at a restaurant, which prompted him to try and distract the officer because he had cocaine, marijuana, and a gun on him. Hoping to somehow avoid the gun being found, he pushed the officer. That resulted in him getting charged with violating his previous parole.

Judy and I were in Carlsbad, California, at one of our time-shares when we received a call from Jasmine telling us Steven was in jail.

We got Steven a lawyer, and he got probation, meaning he could either serve three months in jail, or he could be out of jail and on probation for three months. He chose to serve his time in jail. I think he was afraid that if he broke probation he'd be in worse trouble.

Knowing that Steven was in jail killed us.

Seeing him dressed in prison garb was upsetting. When we visited him, we could tell he was frightened by his surroundings. There were adults in there, but probably not as hardcore as some places. He said he never left his room. He ended up serving 45 days, which was his remaining sentence.

Those days felt like a prison sentence for Judy and me, too.

After Steven got out of jail in June of 2015, he returned home to live with us in his old room, but he had to live by our rules. For example, he had to be home before midnight—we needed decent sleep. We didn't want him smoking weed in the house. And no selling drugs.

Steven seemed to be better for a little while. That gave us a glimmer of hope about his future. We felt a lot more relaxed that he had a place to stay, and that he was in our house with us. I certainly slept a lot better.

At Christmas of 2015, Steven's present to his mother was being able to report that he'd been off cocaine for 60 days. Still, he looked awful at times. That should have been a warning signal. His face would be drooped and he'd just be walking around and out of it. More and more, he would resemble less of the old Steven. He was such a good-looking kid, too. I have a family picture of him at Christmas; he looked terrible. Everybody in the picture looked happy, but his eyes looked funny and his face looked weird. That had to be the drugs.

Because we saw Steven all the time. I think that made gradual changes in him harder to detect. When I saw that Christmas picture, he looked a lot worse than I remembered at the time the photo was taken. That just killed me on the inside. I'd tried to give him direction, and I felt really close to my son.

At Sunday school, I would share my situation with guys who had similar situations. Steven came to church with us a few times.

A friend, Charles Carter, told Steven, "You can fool your dad, but I know you're just talking trash." And we were worried about Steven's faith, because he'd make jokes about God. But Charles told me that Steven had confided in him that he did believe in God.

Charles said, "I think he's trying to make you guys, like, 'get off my back.'"

I constantly prayed for Steven and my daughters, because we always had a prayer circle at our Sunday school class every Sunday. Seemed like I was on my knees all the time.

Unfortunately, Steven still appeared to be dealing drugs.

We suspected he sold drugs from our house because people came by the house in their cars at all hours. We told him we couldn't have that, and if he was going to have people coming to the house at different hours of the day, he could forget about staying with us. We let him know, "Whether you're selling or buying, it ain't going to happen here."

In March of 2016, we kicked him out of the house. He'd never been confrontational. He pretty much went along with whatever we told him. That struck me as kind of sad in a way. He didn't do much protesting. But the fact he couldn't stop having people show up at all hours of the night pressed us to make the decision to kick him out.

We helped him find a place to live. I even paid the deposit.

Steven got hired at Qdoba, a chain Mexican restaurant that is a higher grade than Taco Bell. We found out his bosses really liked him. They said he was a great worker. They said he worked hard all the time, and that he'd do anything for everybody. We thought he was doing well, because he seemed happy when we took him to get some furniture. We bought him a bed at one place. And we'd just bought him a table and lamp from Goodwill. We're thinking he's getting it together. And then boom, that changed.

In April of 2016, we went on a trip out west. When we were on our way home, I texted Steven.

All of the kids were into texts, so Judy and I used texts to keep track of them, even if the text was something simple like, "How are you doing."

I still have the sequence of texts I sent to Steven.

On April 8, 2016:

Me: Are you at work now?

    Steven: Yeah, what's up?

    Me: Just missing you. We're hoping to come back tomorrow (from the West Coast) standby if the weather doesn't stop us. Did you pay your rent yet?

    Steven: Yes

    Me: Was going to look for a lamp and a cheap coffee table. Is the bed comfortable?

Steven: Yes

On April 10, I texted him, but he didn't answer. That prompted me to shoot him a text on April 13:

Me: What are you doing on your day off? You could come and see your mom.

Steven: NO ANSWER

On April 14, Steven came over and he and I went shopping at the Goodwill store. We bought two lamps and a coffee table for his apartment. We went to the house to show his mom the furniture. He said thanks and gave me a strong hug as he left the house.

On April 15, I texted him: Have you gone to Chicago?

I thought he'd gone to Chicago for some reason.

He texted back the same day: No.

So I knew he was okay.

On April 16, I texted him: We're cooking. You still in town? Jasmine is here at the house.

Steven lived at an apartment complex about five miles away. Jasmine wasn't living with us, but she visited us a lot. Steven and she were so close that I suggested he come over while she was with us.

I didn't hear back from him and he wasn't answering his phone. I texted him on April 20: Are you OK?

Steven: NO ANSWER

On April 21, Jasmine called us and said she thought something was wrong, because she wasn't able to contact Steven. We asked Jasmine to go by the apartment to check on him.

When Jasmine got to his apartment, she knocked on his door. Nobody answered. That prompted her to see the landlord to get a key for his apartment. When she got inside, she found him. He'd taken his own life.

Jasmine called me: "Daddy, he's gone."

Judy just about went into shock. I called a neighbor, Natalie Thomas, who lived a couple of houses down, and she stayed with Judy while I went to join Jasmine. I rushed over there right away.

The police wouldn't let me in to see my son. They said it was a bad scene that Jasmine had seen, and we shouldn't go inside. We didn't.

Steven had told people at Qdoba that he was going to Detroit. He'd told them he'd been there before, so we figured he had some friends in Detroit. He missed a shift at Qdoba, and when they called, they couldn't get him, which they said was unusual. They were saddened by his death. They knew he'd struggled with some drug activity.

I don't think Steven ever planned on making that trip to Detroit. I think he'd planned on taking his life all along. In hindsight, I think he'd been fighting depression for a long time.

Jasmine carries a lot of guilt because he'd called her and she hadn't answered. The call he made to her was the last call of his life.

All three of our kids were fighting at the time of Steven's death. Jasmine and Steven weren't fighting. But Julie and Jasmine were fighting. And Julie was upset with Steven, so she felt really guilty about what happened, too.

A memorial for my beautiful son, Bernard Steven Hamilton, III, took place on a Saturday, April 30, 2016, at the First Baptist Church of Jefferson Town. Our pastor Reverend Kevin Nelson conducted the service.

My friend and work colleague, Jackie Austin, planned the memorial. She had been my Christian counseling friend before the tragedy and she remains a close friend today. A Milken finalist and former director of curriculum for the Jefferson County Public Schools, she had also helped me put together the successful African American Male Summit. We had served on the NABSE Board together when she was elected secretary for NABSE. Jackie held my hand and prayed with me for many long days and nights.

NABSE sent national and local people. Their showing was impressive and a nice gesture. The local NABSE people made a quilt with all kinds of comforting words on it. The entire staff from Judy's school came as well.

Back when I'd been president of NABSE, I thought I was in hell when I thought I had to save the organization. But when I lost my son, I experienced a second, and far greater version of hell.

I blamed myself for what happened. I have this spiritual thing that told me I must not have pleased God somewhere along the way. I must have sinned in God's eyes, and losing Steven was God's punishment. And I still feel that way—I didn't do this, I sinned too much, or whatever. Interesting enough, I'm reading the Old Testament every day these days, and there's a lot about, "Okay, you're perfect, but you didn't do this, so I'm taking your first son." Or "I'm not going to let you continue to be king." Those passages bother me a great deal.

Given my upbringing and what I've learned throughout my career in education, and at NABSE, I had tried to do what I could to help save the young Black children of our country. I had tried to be a good role model. But I couldn't save my own son.

## CHAPTER TWENTY-THREE

During the days and weeks that followed Steven's death, I felt lost.

Prior to Steven's death, I'd continued to work to try and help save NABSE's building in by working on a loan for that purpose.

If NABSE didn't get the loan secured by July of 2016, the Wells Fargo Bank had warned us that we would be in default, because we were way overdue, and we hadn't paid our taxes. We needed to come through or we were going to lose our $4 million building on Capitol Hill.

I'd gone through six or seven different companies and I wasn't getting anywhere. I'd gotten down to where I was trying to convince private investors to take a chance on helping to save the building. Eventually, I got in touch with my longtime friend from college, Everett Carolina, aka Slime, the name he'd earned from being such a wheeler-dealer.

I said, "Slime, you think you can help us get this loan?"

Slime came through.

We were at least seven months into trying to make the deal happen when Steven died.

That took me totally out of it, but I had a responsibility to NABSE to see the thing through. Shortly after Steven's funeral, I went back to the phones trying to help make the loan happen. I directed the office to send loan paper, 990 tax forms for nonprofit status. The NABSE building operated two restaurants, so we needed to send along the restaurants' payroll sheets. Along with that, I had to get the board to agree to whatever stipulations they wanted to do for the loan.

Thankfully, we secured the loan in July.

That work helped keep my mind off of Steven's death. I was still trying to save NABSE, even though I'd lost my son. After I'd done so, I felt relief, but I continued to think I can save them, but I couldn't save my son.

In my conversations with God, every night on my knees, I told him back then, and I tell him now, "I'm lost. You have to tell me what to do every day. That's where I'm at every day."

That's when the Lincoln Foundation contacted me and asked me to become their director. When they asked me to take the job, I felt like God had intervened, because the job was all about helping kids.

The Lincoln Foundation provides enrichment for low-income kids. The organization started off being only Black. Now it's totally integrated with 20 different nationalities represented. They provide enrichment, tutoring, and summer training at five different colleges. And they provide $5 million in yearly scholarships to kids. They even give them scholarships while they're in college. The birth of the Lincoln Foundation began with Berea College. A college that has a rich history that included educating Black and White children in an integrated school prior to the Civil War free.

My girls had gone to the Lincoln Foundation for a few summers, because they helped them with their math and science, so I knew a little bit about the foundation. I knew it was an honor to be asked to take the job. I said, "This has to be God. I'll do it."

Taking the job was fabulous for me. And people were kind. I told them I was fragile because of Steven, and that being around kids would be tough. But taking the job turned out to be a road back into the world.

I worked at the Lincoln Foundation until we decided to move from Louisville back to Las Vegas early in 2019.

During our time in Louisville, we helped raise Julie's kids— our two grandchildren. And we continue to try and cope with the loss of our son.

My NABSE experience has been rewarding to me, though I know it has taken a toll on my family.

A lot of that stemmed from my lifelong need to take part in things and help. Remember all those committees and clubs I was a part of while growing up?

I think my kids always thought I was too much—that I was overbearing. I think Judy thought that as well. Many times, I felt as though I was on the outs with my wife and kids. But they reaped some of the benefits of my being involved, and I think I spoiled them. We traveled a lot through NABSE, and they lived the good life. We were in the Disney Hotel. They were around Mickey Mouse, and they got the best of the best. And we flew all over the place. We went to Aruba, Senegal, and the Bahamas. They always lived this great life. Julie got to have dance lessons, tennis lessons, gymnastic lessons, and cheerleading lessons. Jasmine had piano lessons, basketball personal coaching, summer bridge programs, and math tutoring. Steven and Jasmine had me to coach them at the YMCA. Steven also had piano lessons, oboe lessons, baseball coaching, and math tutoring. I wanted to be Superman to them (*I can do all this through him who gives me strength. —Philippians 4:13*).

I always wanted to do more for my family. I felt conflicted. I now realize that along the way I did too much preaching and not enough listening. Judy tried to balance that. I had the old mind-set, "Do as I say, no matter what—even if I'm wrong." Too much preaching and not enough listening. Kids of principals and teachers, they kind of rebel.

Somewhere along the way Judy and I began to go to counseling, and I told her I probably should have gone sooner. She had wanted us to go before.

Judy and I have always had strong opinions, and not necessarily ones we agreed about. She's a pretty strong person, well educated, and a leader, no doubt. She is a licensed clinical counselor as well as a school counselor. Prominent people would ask her to counsel them. In the church she had gone to, she was the marriage counselor couples were required to visit before the preacher would marry them. She also did sessions for kids at the church before they got into trouble.

Ironically, after all the problems with our kids, our marriage actually got better. And I don't know if it was because I softened or she had nowhere else to go. I was the only one she had. She even stopped going to her church and started going to mine. She had been going to a larger church that had different programs that she liked.

We relied on our faith quite a bit.

Today, I still consult with NABSE. We have a past presidents' council. The past presidents meet at all the national conferences and we talk about what we can do to help.

Probably the main thing that needs to happen is for NABSE's governing board to be more educated on their role as a board and the responsibilities of a nonprofit. I don't think they ever understood that completely. And there also needs to be some more accountability and consequences when protocols are not followed. For example, there should never be a time when their IRS paperwork isn't done. They should always have a timely audit. They should not incur expenses that they can't afford.

The biggest problem NABSE has had for probably 15 years or more is that it spent the money before they received it. Every year they depended on one big conference as their main source of income. That worked well as long as we weren't in the middle of a recession and the conferences were well managed, because they had a surplus of money. If that didn't happen, they'd be in trouble.

The need to secure solid funding from the membership still remains a barrier. The board members, officers, and staff should survey the membership yearly, maintain consistent communication them, and have ongoing training for all NABSE officers. That would provide a continuity that would build on the positive foundation that past founders and officers have provided NABSE.

Mind you, I have not been president for several years now, and NABSE continues to try and catch up. But they'll get there.

I'm pleased with a lot of what I've been able to accomplish, or help get accomplished, at NABSE. It's like a good coach. If you can put in a good foundation that others can follow, then you feel like you've done something. NABSE will be fine. It will always have its issues, but it will be okay.

A long time ago, I chose to live a faith-based life, and I got involved with NABSE, because I liked what the organization represented and the direction it seemed to be heading.

My faith continues to hold me together. I talk to many people who have lost someone. Some will tell me they're mad at God. I've never been able to feel mad. I'm more like, "How did I disappoint you?"

My whole mission in life has been to try and get something stable that could save the kids. I always felt like I was saved but so many others haven't been saved, and need to be saved. I just feel so bad for them.

I just credit my holding on to faith. And focusing on that. I have had a hard time. I'm constantly asking myself what am I doing to make the situation better. I feel guilty all the time, and sad about that. It's tough. I know I'm blessed to have gone through what I did growing up and being where I'm at today. I think I have survival guilt.

I've invested my life in NABSE and my faith. My work with NABSE, as with every job, also benefited from my praying colleagues and relatives. Today I feel good about our efforts. There had been many hard pursuits, but worthwhile things are hard.

NABSE is the nation's premier nonprofit organization devoted to furthering the academic success for all children, particularly children of African descent.

The organization functions through its affiliates and its job like commissions. Information about NABSE can be accessed through its website at www.nabse.org.

Listed below are the 2014 NABSE affiliates and the presidents of those affiliates as they existed during my term as NABSE president. They are listed state by state within their designated regions; the president's name is listed below the affiliate's name. Also listed are the commissions and the chairpersons that served during my term of office.

# 2014 NABSE AFFILIATES

## NORTHEAST REGION

### CONNECTICUT

Great New England ABSE
Cassandra Butler

### DELAWARE

Greater Delaware ABSE
Phyllise Wilkins-Church

Delaware ABSE
Kendal Mobley

## MARYLAND

Maryland ABSE
Vanessa Bass

Anne Arundel County ABSE
Don Lilley

Baltimore County ABSE
Brian C. Morrison

Hartford County ABSE
Shirley W. Faulkner

Metro Baltimore ABSE
Velma Hicks

Montgomery County ABSE
Charles Feamster

Prince Georges County ABSE
Anthony A. Fears

Washington County ABSE
Brenda J. Thlam

## MASSACHUSETTS

Black Educators of Massachusetts
Ms. Nora L. Toney

## NEW JERSEY

Greater Newark ABSE
Brenda R. Lee

## NEW YORK

ABSE of New York
Mellouise Murdaugh

Central New York ABSE
Ernest Wood

Long Island ABSE
Brenday Joyce "Brandy" Scott

Metropolitan Buffalo ABSE
W. Charles Brandy

Mount Vernon ABSE
Ann Berkley

New York ABSE
Brenda Canty

Ossining ABSE
Jerry O. Norris

Rockland ABSE
Pierre Gay
**New York (Continued)**

State University of New York
at Oswego ABSE
Channel Lindsay

Westchester ABSE
Charles L. Jones

## PENNSYLVANIA

Greater Pittsburg ABSE
Wayne Walters

Philadelphia Affiliate ABSE
Angela Gilbert

DVA-NABSE
Crystal Dowdell

## SOUTHEAST REGION

### ALABAMA

Birmingham ABSE
Steve Brown

### FLORIDA

Broward County ABSE
Carletha B. Shaw

Greater Tallahassee ABSE
Melinda Jackson

Hillsborough Area ABSE
Mary Dance

Jacksonville ABSE
Catherine L. Barnes

Miami ABSE
Beverly Carter-Remy

Orlando ABSE
Marvia Barrington

Pinellas ABSE
Teresa Anderson

Polk ABSE
Terry Strong

### GEORGIA

Atlanta Metro ABSE
Thelma Muford-Glover

## KENTUCKY

Greater Louisville ABSE
Adrian L. Layne

Blue Grass ABSE
Elaine Farris

Kentucky ABSE
D'Artagnan Ramsey

Lexington ABSE
Donna George

## MISSISSIPPI

Mississippi ABSE
Earl Watkins

## NORTH CAROLINA

Greater Charlotte ABSE
Eva Cooper

North Carolina ABSE
Marvin Connelly

Wayne County ABSE
Betty Howell Gray

## SOUTH CAROLINA

South Carolina ABSE
Nathaniel Hayes

## TENNESSEE

Greater Nashville ABSE
Donnie Crenshaw

Memphis ABSE
Jeffrey Akins

## VIRGINIA

Charlottesville Albemarie ABSE
Wes Bellamy

Fairfax County ABSE
Malicia Braxton

Prince William ABSE
Andrea Sparks-Brown

Richmond Area ABSE
William Joyner

Tidewater ABSE
Olivia Dabney

## SOUTHWEST

## ARKANSAS

Arkansas ABSE
Lloyd Sain, Jr.

## KANSAS

Kansas ABSE
Melba Underwood

## LOUISIANA

Jefferson ABSE
Carol Turner

Greater New Orleans ABSE
Wanda D. Brooks

New Orleans ABSE
H. Kenneth Johnston

## MISSOURI

Greater Kansas City ABSE
Edward Underwood

Metropolitan St. Louis ABSE
Patricia Jones

## OKLAHOMA

Oklahoma City Metro ABSE
Gilbert Oliver

Tulsa Area ABSE
James Jones

## TEXAS

Texas ABSE
John W. Washington

Alamo Area ABSE
Theodore R. Haynes, Jr.

Arlington Area ABSE
Grace Alaman

Austin Area ABSE
Linelle Clark Brown

Bastrop Area ABSE
Charlie C. Haynes

Beaumont Area ABSE
Sybel Comeaux

Brazos Area ABSE
Kristiana Hamilton

Consolidated ABSE
Christopher McCall

Corpus Christi Area ABSE
La Tricia Johnson

Dallas Regional ABSE
Marian A. Willard

Denton Area ABSE
Tracy Baines

East Texas Area ABSE

Shirley Davis

Fort Worth ABSE
Khaleiah Taylor

Galveston ABSE
Maxine Guidry

Garland Area ABSE
Edwin P. Hood

Golden Crescent ABSE
Laura Holcombe

Houston Area ABSE
Dawn DuBose Randle

Killeen Area ABSE
SheWanda O. Blackman

Lubbock Area ABSE
Glenda Cook

Prairie View A&M ABSE
Angela Dickson

Texas Southern University ABSE
Teryana Lamb

West Central Texas ABSE
Allan Nell Lockett

# MIDWEST REGION

## ILLINOIS

Chicago Area ABSE
Jeffery Dase

Rockford ABSE
Glenda Hildreth

South Suburban Chicago ABSE
Leotis D. Swopes

## INDIANA

Fort Wayne ABSE
Charles E. Green

Indianapolis ABSE
Michael Chisley

Northwest Indiana ABSE
Jacquelyn (Jacky) Gholson

## IOWA

Iowa ABSE
Mary Lynne Jones

## MICHIGAN

Greater Lansing Area ABSE
Sonya Gunnings-Morton

Metropolitan Detroit ABSE

Deanna Hunt

Southwest Michigan ABSE
Nkenge Bergan

## MINNESOTA

Minnesota ABSE
Francine Chakolis

## OHIO

Ohio ABSE
Jeannette Henson

Akron ABSE
Johnette S. Curry

Cleveland Heights ABSE
Michelle D. Walton

Franklin County ABSE
Jesse L. Jackson

Greater Cincinnati ABSE
Amy Jones Harrigan

Lelia Green ABSE
Sandy Womack

Lorain County ABSE
Joy Jones

Ohio (Continued)

Metro Cleveland ABSE
Laverne Hooks

Sandusky Area ABSE
Fran Cox

Springfield Area ABSE
James Williams

Toledo ABSE
Desire Carn

Youngstown ABSE
Ralph Goldston

## WISCONSIN

Metropolitan Milwaukee ABSE
Nuntiata Buck


## WEST REGION


## ARIZONA

Arizona ABSE
Zelatrice Fowler

Tucson ABSE
Herman House

## CALIFORNIA

California ABSE

Sandy Carpenter-Stevenson

Elk Grove ABSE
BernNadette Best-Green

High Desert ABSE
Gwendolynne Y. Cole

Inland Empire ABSE
Noaveyar Daily

Los Angeles County ABSE
Derotha Williams

Oakland ABSE
Clifford Thomas

Pomona ABSE
Linda Ursery-Fleming

Ravenswood ABSE
Marti Hargrove

San Francisco ABSE
Tareyton Russ

Santa Clara County ABSE
Leon Beauchman

Valley Alliance of African American Educators
Phillip Abode

California (Continued)

Victory Valley
Alaric Singletary

## NEVADA

Las Vegas ABSE
Ana Lee

## OREGON

Oregon ABSE
Keylah Boyer Frazier

## WASHINGTON

Seattle ABSE
Ina Howell

Washington ABSE
Patricia Mon Cure Thomas

## <u>INTERNATIONAL</u>

## BERMUDA

Bermuda ABSE
Melvyn Bassett

## BAHAMAS

Nassau ABSE
Sheila Culmer

## CANADA

Nova Scotia ABSE
Jaqueline Smith-Herriott

Ontario ABSE
Warren Salmon

## COMMISSIONS IN 2014

Instructional Support Commission
Melba Underwood

District Commission
Lois Johnson

Superintendent Commission
Tony Sawyer

Governance Commission
Lynda Jackson

Parent Commission
Gloria Funches

Higher Education Commission
Steve McLary

Retired Commission
Joan Kelly

Made in the USA
San Bernardino, CA
01 March 2020

65201534R00175